TRAGIC REDEMPTION

To Janet and Del,
His grace is
Sufficient!

TRAGIC REDEMPTION:
Healing the Guilt and Shame

Hiram Johnson

Foreword by Stephen A. Seamands

LANGMARC
PUBLISHING
AUSTIN, TEXAS

TRAGIC REDEMPTION:
Healing the Guilt and Shame

By Hiram Johnson

Cover painting: Jullie Hunley
Cover by Michael Qualben

Bible quotations taken from *The New International Version*
(NIV) of the Bible are used by permission.

PUBLISHED BY
LANGMARC PUBLISHING
P. O. 90488
AUSTIN, TEXAS 78709-0488

Library of Congress Control Number: 2006922014
ISBN: 1-880292-777

DEDICATION

This book is written in honor and memory of
Athena (Tina) Watson.

It is also dedicated to my whole family and
in honor and memory of my parents,
Cecil and Sue Johnson-Neville.
I miss you and love you very much.

TABLE OF CONTENTS

ACKNOWLEDGMENTS

I express my deepest gratitude and appreciation to my dear wife, Jill, for all of her support, patience, and love in helping get this book published. She is simply the best! A special thank you to my daughters, Hannah and Sarah, for loving their daddy and for allowing me to stay on the computer for countless hours.

I thank Dr. Myron Madden, Dr. Steve Seamands, and Diane Bekurs for their invaluable assistance with the manuscript. A special thank you to my editors, Dr. Bonnie Harvey and Betty Whitworth, for all their guidance, feedback, and suggestions. Thank you to Jullie Hunley for her excellent work on the book's cover, and to Pam Denham for her outstanding role as the book's formal publicist. Also, thank you to Lois Qualben at LangMarc Publishing for continuing to believe in the original manuscript.

Thank you to my sister Donna Wells and her husband, Col. Mark Wells, for their insights and input. Thank you to my step-father, Bud Neville, for his words of wisdom and encouragement. Also, a heartfelt thank you to Paul and Ruth Adams, the best in-laws a man could possibly have, for all of their help, too. They are the prototype of parents. I have always admired their deep faith.

God has truly blessed me with such wonderful people. I thank God, most of all, for delivering me from the depths of tragedy. I am strong only because of His never ending grace.

FOREWORD

Simone Weil (1909-1943), the brilliant French philosopher and activist, grew up in an agnostic Jewish home but later was drawn to Christianity especially because of its profound view of human suffering. "The extreme greatness of Christianity," she maintained, "lies in the fact that it does not seek a supernatural *remedy* for suffering but a supernatural *use* for it."

In the Christian scheme of things, as exemplified most profoundly in Christ's death on the cross, God's solution to the problems of suffering and evil is not to eliminate it or to be insulated from it, but to participate in it and then transform it into his instrument for redemption of the world. Rather than hindering God's work, God takes the tragedy of Christ's death—the evil, the injustice, the pain—and turns it into a triumph. He weaves it into his redemptive plan for the salvation of fallen creation.

The cross, the central symbol of Christianity, thus demonstrates that even when things have gone tragically wrong, God can still use our anguish creatively to bring blessings out of it that could not have been achieved any other way. In fact, this is God's way of redemption; this is how God, in the face of the evil and suffering in our lives, works to accomplish his will and his purposes in us and through us. He takes our garbage and recycles it. He transforms our places of humiliation and shame into our places of spiritual authority. The title of this book—*Tragic Redemption*—captures it well. This is God's method: to take our tragedies and redeem them.

But instead of offering us an abstract theological description of the wonder of divine redemption (as I have just sought to do), what Hiram Johnson does in the pages that follow is much more compelling. As he unfolds his own personal story of tragic redemption, we are given a profound personal "in living color" example of how God's method is actually worked out in human life and experience. As a result of his graphic, engaging account, the principle of tragic redemption, demonstrated as it is in the life of a person, now takes on a human face. The abstract becomes concrete; the verbal becomes vital. Indeed, the flesh and blood picture we are given here is worth a thousand words and more.

Hiram's story focuses on a particular tragedy in his own life: his involvement in a fatal accident involving a young woman who was a passenger in the car he was driving. The profound guilt and shame he experienced as a result of this caused him to descend into alcoholism, depression, despair, and attempted suicide.

But Hiram does much more than simply recount his story. As he describes his downward spiral in vivid detail, at various points he steps back and reflects upon the psychological and spiritual dynamics of his experience. It was at these points that I found him most helpful. His insightful analysis of the various dimensions of guilt and shame, his honest grappling with his own pride and desire to be in control, his description of his struggle in accepting God's forgiveness combine to make this a valuable resource for us all but especially for those living under a dark, heavy cloud of guilt and shame.

In describing the way God carried him through the dark times and then worked to redeem his tragedy, I appreciate the honest realism of Hiram's account. If you are looking for quick-fix solutions to your problems, you won't find them here. His journey in overcoming guilt and shame and receiving divine grace was slow and arduous—one that required much courage and determination. Sometimes three steps forward were followed by two steps backward.

Yet through it all, God was faithful in providing the strength and the encouragement, the wisdom and insight, the patience and persistence Hiram needed to stay on the path toward healing. This book, then, is a marvelous testimony to the God who pursues us with his grace and relentless love, and the One who works together in all things for good to those who love him and are called according to his purpose (Romans 8:28). Hiram's place of greatest guilt and shame has indeed become a place of spiritual authority in his life and thus a means of blessing to us all. His story of tragic redemption will move you to give praise and glory to God.

Stephen A. Seamands
Professor of Christian Doctrine
Asbury Theological Seminary
Wilmore, Kentucky
Author of *Wounds that Heal* and
Ministry in the Image of God.

- 1 -

THE ACCIDENT

Suddenly, the laughter stopped. The ensuing silence was eerie and deafening, followed by the awful smell of cold steel. In the midst of the silence, my first conscious thought was, "What have I done now...?" Then I heard Mike's faint voice call, "Can you get out?" I was disoriented and felt excruciating pain in my left arm, which had been broken in half by the steering wheel. Broken glass was embedded in my scalp; I felt encased in shattered glass. Instinctively, I reached down with my broken arm and jarred the crumpled door open. When I saw my white sweater turn crimson from my blood, I thought I was dying.

One of my friends in the back seat ran to a nearby home and called for ambulances. My remaining memories of that night came from the physical perspective of lying on the ground, writhing in extreme pain, and looking skyward. I was shivering, but it was more out of fear than the chilled night air. I could vividly see the stars but could hear only the horrible sounds of something gone terribly wrong: wailing sirens, car doors opening and closing, and people's rapid footsteps approaching the scene. The reflections of the swirling red lights and ambulance headlights made strange patterns in the surrounding treetops. I could even smell the salt in the night air from the nearby gulf waters. Because of the intense pain, my heels had dug small trenches into the lifeless ground. In spite of the pain, I felt paralyzed from the waist up. All I could do was frantically kick. A woman knelt beside me and kept telling me, "Hold on. Help is on the way."

Two friends trapped in the front seat of the now-totaled car were being released by the "jaws of life." That chilling sound is one I will never forget. Mike, sitting next to me, suffered a dislocated hip and a broken leg, which required multiple surgeries. His gait would be permanently affected. Another young man in the front seat, sustained cracked ribs, cuts, and bruises. A walk-on at a major college football program, his mammoth size actually insulated him from more serious injuries. Two men in the back seat were only slightly injured, while one of the two young women later needed corrective dental work and had to wear a supportive brace on her injured ankle. But the other girl, Tina, a 17-year-old senior, lapsed into a coma that night. Initially, I was told that she was conscious after the impact. One of the men in the back seat asked her if she was OK. She nodded yes and said she just needed to lay her head down. When she did so, she lost consciousness.

Later, as I was rushed inside the emergency room, I could hear the churning helicopter blades transporting Tina to a larger, more extensive hospital in nearby Pensacola. Hospital personnel cut my blood-soaked clothes off of me. I was bleeding in more places than I realized. Then I saw my parents' shocked and frightened faces looking down at me trying to offer any means of support and encouragement. I don't remember any other words spoken that night—by me or any others—it was like seeing disjointed frames from a horrific silent movie reel.

For a college junior being home from Florida State University for the Christmas holidays in 1979 meant having a good time. On the Tuesday night of December 18, 1979, my friend Mike and I enjoyed a basketball game at our alma mater high school in Niceville, a small town nestled in the Florida panhandle. Once there we got together with some other friends. After the game, we decided to meet at Lincoln Park just across the bay. Because of the frigid temperature, everyone—five young men and two young women—got into my parents' 1968 Pontiac Catalina, which I was driving. This car gave us more room to talk and catch up on everyone's activities.

Mike and I had just met the two high school girls. Because the basketball game went into overtime, we had gotten out late. It was almost 11:00 P.M. by the time all of us arrived at the park. After talking for about thirty minutes, we decided to go to a convenience store located less than a mile away. On the drive there, Mike, both girls, and I sat in the front seat, which resulted in overcrowding. My arms felt too restricted while driving the car. Before leaving the store, we talked a few minutes in the parking lot, and we decided to change to having three people in the front seat. Because of my request, the two girls moved to the back, trading places with one of the guys. Little did I know my simple and innocent request would actually make matters worse.

As we drove back to the park, tragedy struck. I was driving about 35 miles per hour on a twisting, bayside road when one of the guys in the front seat told a joke about a rival college football team. We all started to laugh, and I laughed so hard I took my eyes off of the road for a split second causing the car to veer off the gradual left turn. We crashed head on into a massive oak tree, just two feet from the road. It happened so fast, I didn't even think of brakes, much less to use them. None of us knew what happened or what had hit us; but chance had cruelly met us.

"...No man knows when his hour will come: As fish are caught in a cruel net, or birds are taken in a snare, so men are trapped by evil times that fall unexpectedly upon them" (Ecclesiastes 9:12).

I knew Tina had been taken to the hospital, but I received no official word about her condition. I asked the doctors every day if she was doing better, and I repeatedly prayed for her recovery. The week was very long and grueling as I waited for what had to be good news. Each day Tina survived, I assumed she became stronger and more likely to recover. I wouldn't let myself think of any other scenario. One week later, on Christmas Day, Tina died from head injuries, having never regained consciousness. She suffered multiple blood clots in the brain from apparently striking the roof of the car. None of us had been wearing seat belts.

My doctor thought it best that I not learn of Tina's death until my condition stabilized. I was formally listed in guarded condition. In the meantime, I needed additional surgery on Christmas morning because of a post-operative infection in my arm. I would later require four operations to mend the fractures and infection.

A few days later, while still in ICU, I was emotionally shattered when told of Tina's death. I can still hear the doctor's stunning words: "I've got some bad news; I'm sorry, but the girl didn't make it..." I felt completely empty, numb, and blank. At first, I could not speak, breathe, nor even cry. I sensed an ever-darkening, dreadful haze around me. The wind and my very soul had been knocked out of me.

How could Tina's family cope with such devastating news? How could I ever overcome this tragedy? On Christmas Day? Please let this accident be some kind of mistake. I felt Tina's family would have to "celebrate" Christmas with a solemn black wreath forever. Moreover, her death and funeral had taken place before I even found out. I was the sole cause of her death but selfishly felt shut out of the formal grieving process. Now, I wanted to scream and cry out as loud and as long as I could, but it seemed the window of opportunity had closed. It would be very difficult to grieve the death of a virtual stranger who had died by my own hands. Racing thoughts and fears continued to accelerate and kept my mind spinning.

The extent of each person's injuries was another strange and peculiar aspect of that night. One person suffered from only a bloody nose, and the person sitting right next to him died. Only inches and seconds determined our fate. In a sense, we are all one second, one phone call, or one seat away from adversity.

During this time, I was terrified to think of the feelings Tina's family might have toward me. How could I ever show my shameful face to them? And because Tina's death so overwhelmed me, I failed to focus on the other families involved. Even though their children had been injured in varying degrees, I didn't immediately follow up in expressing my sorrow to them. One of their children could have been the one who died. Eventually, I was relieved to know that no one in the car or any of their family members held any animosity toward me. Although grateful, it still didn't bring me any significant solace for the death of Tina.

I took my eyes off the road for a mere instant. Simple carelessness had led to someone's death. This had to be a terror-filled nightmare from which I would awaken. Nevertheless, I was in a harsh and cruel reality instead of a nightmare that would soon end. As in any accident and sudden death, I was in a state of emotional shock, bewildered by the speed and severity of it all; I wanted the instant back. I was careless, not deliberate in intending to hurt anyone. Surely someone would allow me to make amends by giving me a second chance, but I didn't find any takers.

The only thing I could do was apologize. "I am so sorry," seemed so inadequate. Any regret on my part could not possibly atone for someone's death. Part of me felt a mere apology would be nothing short of an insult. "Sorry" sounded like such a weak word. No words in the English language brought me any relief. In fact, words kept getting in the way of what I wanted to say or feel. I just needed time to feel remorse and not have anyone push anything like hope on me too soon. Hope would have to wait. At this pivotal juncture, I had absolutely no interest. I just needed a Presence in the pain and some direction in the darkness. But this was a valley I didn't want to walk through, much less acknowledge its existence. Psalm 23:4 tells us, "Even though I walk through the valley of the shadow of death, I will fear no evil, for you are with me."

While recovering in ICU, I vividly remember Pastor Doug Newton and his son Allen visiting Mike, who had been sitting next to me in the car. Mike was a member of their church. The pastor made a point to visit with me as well. Although he did not know our family, he sat with my parents for hours during my initial surgery. That night God's spirit was already ministering to each of us through this wonderful man. A strong bond and relationship between him and our family was forged. In short, he became a dear friend. Through him, I began to see and experience my first glimpses of God since the tragedy.

I still could not and would not accept what had happened. Someone died, and I caused her death. If it weren't for me, Tina would be alive. What a devastating feeling! I knew it was an accident, but as the driver I felt morally responsible for her death as well as for the others' injuries.

I was legally responsible, too. A few days later, the city police chief formally charged me with careless driving and fined me $35. The chief knew many of us growing up in such a small town. He was the president of our local little league. His tearful, caring eyes and words showed me that he and the entire community were shaken by this tragedy, too. He said the seriousness of the accident results dictated that I had to be charged. I understood completely and tearfully signed the ticket from my hospital bed. The local newspaper's bold headline the next day, "MAN CHARGED IN FATAL ACCIDENT," virtually cemented my self-imposed fate as a careless outcast.

Adding to the madness and hysteria of such a tragic event, painful rumors began to spread throughout our community. Many people assumed I was drunk, speeding, or that drugs were involved. None of these rumors were true, but the quiet glances and whispers hurt. We had alcohol in the car, but after the interviews and the performance of the appropriate tests, the police confirmed that alcohol was not a factor. The accident was alcohol related in the sense it was the primary reason we went to the convenience store. But those details would not change the deadly outcome. I realize the natural assumption many people, including myself, may make when you mention youth, car accident, and alcohol in the same conversation. People can really let you down by what they say behind your back. A rumor is an anonymous hurt with no accountability, because it has no discernible source. This is a given, dark side of human nature, but it was a struggle to detach and disengage from these rumors and not take them personally. Instead, I internalized the hurtful words, which created more inner anger and resentment. Paul Tournier writes, "The pleasure in gossip and scandal answers to this need of feeling oneself less isolated and alone with one's own repressed guilt by emphasizing other people's guilt."[1]

One aspect of God's grace is forbearance, which means "to bear with each other." Patience is the capacity to bear trials calmly while remaining steadfast despite opposition or adversity. Forbearance literally means "to put up with." Neither forbearance nor patience was a spiritual gift of mine at this dark hour. Later by receiving God's forgiveness through Christ, I forfeited the right to be offended when others hurt me. Even so, practicing and applying the admonition of the Apostle Paul is still sometimes a very tough thing to do.

It would be the greatest understatement in the world to say that fateful night would change everyone involved in the accident. My physical position of sitting behind the steering wheel would radically change my entire existence—physically, emotionally, and spiritually. Those few precious, fleeting seconds of misjudgment and carelessness started me on a path that would ultimately bring me to accept Christ and God's healing grace, but it would be a very long and tortuous journey.

"...but we will all be changed." I Corinthians 15:51

-2-

THE IMMEDIATE AFTERMATH

"Then He said to them. 'My soul is overwhelmed with sorrow to the point of death. Stay
here and keep watch with me.'"

Matthew 26:38

Two weeks later, upon my discharge from the hospital, I learned more harrowing news. Tina's father had
died three years before in a car accident at the age of 41.
Tina's mother and family were going through the depths
of hell once again. What a surreal and incredulous time.
Upon arriving home, I called Tina's mother and asked if
I could come over and talk. She was very gracious in
accepting my request to visit. I had to go into that home
with its atmosphere of unbearable grief. Accompanied
by my parents, I met Tina's mother and explained in
minute detail what had happened that night. This wasn't
a courageous act on my part, as several people told me
later; I just had to do the right thing. Righteousness
doesn't necessarily require courage. After telling Tina's
mother all the specific details and expressing my heart-

felt sorrow, I slowly walked across the living room into
her open arms. Asking Tina's mother to forgive me was
one of the toughest things I have ever done. Only forgiving myself would be more formidable. Through her
tears, compassion, and understanding, she had the power
and willingness to forgive me. We hugged each other,
and she comforted me. After all this precious woman
had gone through, she was comforting me. "Never does
the human soul appear so strong and noble as when it
forgoes revenge and dares to forgive injury" writes
Edwin Hubbel Chapin.

Although appreciative and grateful for Tina's
mother's response, I continued to feel guilty and
ashamed. There is no doubt God was with us that day,
although the feelings of deep sorrow overwhelmed His
spiritual presence. Indeed, it was a time to weep. In the
back of my mind, I thought I would never recover or
come to terms with this tragic event. I kept waiting to
wake up from the world's worst nightmare, but I never
did.

To make matters worse, I became further frustrated
when people tried to help me. Telling me not to rely on
my own understanding certainly didn't bring any comfort. All Scripture is pure and true, but the timing and
context in which it is read or heard makes the difference
as to whether it is significant, embraced, or from our
current perspective, just feels downright cruel. I rushed
to find a meaningful answer, but only became disappointed in the feelings Scripture initially brought.

Hope

"In forgiveness, our behavior is no longer dominated or controlled by old guilt but by new hope."
James Mayfield

At this point, I reluctantly began the elusive quest for hope. Through the adversity, maybe hope was the only choice to make. We keep and cultivate hope in anticipation of great things to come. Hope is a form of trust and reliability and can be a lighthouse in the midst of rough waters. Hope is not in us, but in God and His people. Hope also provides a vision of redemption in the midst of our suffering. The possibility of transformation forms the essence of hope. Gabriel Marcel states, "Hope is a memory of the future." Christ's resurrection from the darkness of death is our basis of hope in the midst of tragedy (Acts 2:23-36).

Adversity can kill hope and compel a person to be in despair or to give up. Often it is the quantity and quality of suffering that dashes any reasonable human basis for hope. Suffering and the power of hope are inevitable. If our confidence in God breaks down, we face the loss of hope and the victory of meaningless suffering. Charles Spurgeon points out, "It is from the grace of God that all hope begins. Grace must reign, or man must die. All other roads are broken up; grace alone bridges the chasm to man and makes a way for traffic between heaven and earth."[1]

Hope was too confusing to me. I couldn't hope for Tina's return, and I felt too guilty to hope for myself. Besides, I had no real concept of hope in a God I didn't know. Hope can be a precarious thing to someone who is suffering and lacks a personal relationship with Christ. Initially, hope was just another stranger awkwardly shoved into my life. My hopelessness produced perplexing feelings of being crushed and entrapped. It felt like hope was an unknown entity waiting just around the corner to kill and destroy me. What made it worse was the feeling that it would last a lifetime. But in the light of hope, suffering can be endured and managed.

The most important aspect is whether we succeed or fail to relate suffering and hope to each other. In a sense, my suffering was just. I was responsible, but even so, I felt a sense of unfairness. I felt torn in opposite directions, feeling caught between the dimensions of responsibility and of having made what normally is an insignificant mistake—had it not resulted in devastating consequences.

> "The gospel of God's suffering love in Christ is inseparable from the gospel of hope, in fact Christians anticipate the celebration of the defeat of the power of death. The Cross points to the necessity of suffering, not to its nobility."[2]
>
> Christian Beker

Spiraling Downward

In the spring, after all of my physical injuries healed, I tried to go back to college. I voluntarily gave up my life-long dream of becoming a pilot by requesting and receiving a medical discharge from the Air Force Reserve. I wanted nothing to do with even the potential of being linked to a person's death ever again. Then, my concentration level and academic performance rapidly declined. In short, I was an emotional mess spiraling out of control. Guilt had more than just a mere grip on me. One of my biggest mistakes after the tragedy was my unwillingness to talk about it.

Any pain, emotional or physical, is allowed by God to guide us to integration; integration ultimately makes us stronger. Just because God allows pain does not mean He causes it. Integration is the process of absorbing our experiences into a functioning whole. Our wholeness thus incorporates both the good and the bad and is a totality of all our experiences. When something is integral, it is essential to completeness.

Although I was not aware of it, Jesus had begun to change me, layer by layer, into a new creation, one with a brand new nature. I had just started and still am in the process of becoming new and whole—warts, flaws, quirks, scars, skills, talents, and all.

Pride and ignorance in handling the guilt and shame became my worst enemy. It was my problem, and it was going to be my solution. I stiff-armed reality from the emotional pain, but also from the help and love I so desperately needed. By isolating myself emotionally, I became an uncharted island in the middle of a vast, lonely sea. My need to control on my terms became what controlled me. Also, many unidentified feelings produced a false sense of safety and self-righteousness, which actually covered the guilt. And I didn't want anyone taking my covers.

At this point, many people suggested counseling, but I adamantly refused. Naivety and immaturity led me to believe that counseling was for weak, emotionally-crippled people, and that no complete stranger could possibly help me. 1 Corinthians 13:11 aptly describes my reasoning at this time, "When I was a child, I talked like a child, I thought like a child, I reasoned like a child."

In regard to the accident, I wish I could be so noble as to say my anger was directed toward God, but it was primarily directed toward myself. I felt complete self-contempt and disgust, sickened, and ashamed by my behavior and very existence. I also came to the brutal awareness that I was angry at Tina for dying. Although we barely knew each other, she had abandoned me in death. Even though it was obviously not her decision to leave, I felt abandoned. She wasn't supposed to die. I felt more guilt because I was still alive to suffer. Then, more guilt ensued for being angry at someone who was the

victim of my own actions. These self-described embarrassing and humiliating insights led me to stuff the
"abnormal and sick" feelings. Was someone's death not
enough? By potentially sharing these feelings, I feared it
would be disloyal and disrespectful to Tina's memory.

Chronic flashbacks and nightmares continued to be
the norm. Although my mind kept reliving that horrible
night, Tina kept dying. Even when I awoke from the
nightmares, it took many fearful moments to realize it
was a dream and not reality. On the other hand, at times
I preferred the terrifying dreams over reality. Reality
was quickly becoming more unbearable than the tor-
menting nightmares.

A part of me died the moment the doctor told me
those stunning words about Tina's death. His words
would also ultimately lead me to a more important
death and rebirth. In a healthy, spiritual way, my old
self would need to die. But at the same time, I felt as if
Tina's death would surely haunt me forever, and living
through this grueling ordeal would be my lifelong curse.
Other obsessive thoughts included: maybe if the tree
had been farther away from the road—maybe if the joke
had been an instant sooner or later or maybe if Tina had
been sitting somewhere else in the car. There were
virtually hundreds of agonizing "ifs," "should haves,"
and "if onlys." "If onlys," however, never change what is.

Human beings have an innate need to blame
someone or something in order to try to understand and
cope with tragedy. But blame games wear thin. Finding
fault is not necessarily a key to healing. Not to duck
accountability, I had to move from blame to belief.
Without any doubt, responsibility for the accident started
and ended with me. There was never any form of hedging
on my part. But blame was becoming irrelevant to the
outcome. It was my fault, but what should I do now? My

response would soon become the most significant issue. The "if onlys" lived and thrived in the past and were fixated on things I couldn't change. They were laced with regret, bitterness, and blame and were primary ingredients in my increasing depression. Giving up my "if onlys" would be one of the most profound sacrifices I could make. We defeat their power not by changing the past but by changing our current perspective(s).

Accountability and acceptance would help me move into the present. It was difficult to accept an outcome I didn't understand or agree with. Accepting is not condoning nor is it a form of disloyalty to anyone. These were feelings I had while struggling with this issue. Accepting someone's death is the highest form of loyalty to both the deceased and to God. For us to move on is the way we can best honor, celebrate, and give meaning to the deceased person's life and death. Too many times we allow someone's death to have more influence over us than their life. Moving on is a conscious choice to continue with life. Our faith and memories allow the deceased to live within our hearts and minds forever. Remember when Jesus stared death in the eye, it was death that blinked.

Accepting, forgiving, and healing are all involved in the slow, complex process of integrating our pain and despair. We need to take our time. When we accept, we regard an event as having a certain meaning, and we take hold of and assume an obligation for it. Our internal processes will need to involve other people. We should never underestimate the power and presence of a compassionate spoken word. God speaks to us through another person's presence and words, but being patient in pain is contrary to our human nature. Many times our mindset doesn't want anything to do with acceptance. For a long time, I compared acceptance to cowardly giving up.

-3-

The Role of Alcoholism

"Do not get drunk on wine, which leads to
debauchery. Instead, be filled with the Spirit."

Ephesians 5:18

Slowly, my depression deepened. To compound the
problem, alcohol became a form of escape. I simply
could not deal with the overwhelming guilt and shame
on a conscious level. But "medicating" myself through
drinking certainly didn't help in the long run. It made
the problem worse by pushing the agonizing emotions
deeper into my unconscious. During these difficult times,
I found that a few hours without pain (however attained) was a huge tradeoff, regardless of any long-term
consequences. Any behavior, functional or dysfunctional, has a positive intent, although I was not aware of
it.

Like any other addiction, alcohol "worked" for a
limited time. In the shortest of terms, it brought a sense
of relief by temporarily lifting my mood. Because I grew

up with an alcoholic father and I was not a Christian, I
knew of no other way to deal with the emotional pain.
But being raised in an alcoholic background was no
excuse. All people drink for the same reason. They
choose to drink. At this point, I didn't care, nor was I
aware of the eventual consequences. Although alcohol,
like any other addiction, may dull our emotional pain, it
also dulls our passion for God.

Alcohol and food are the two biggest tranquilizers
we use today. What makes them so potentially dangerous is their accessibility and acceptability. We have an
oral fixation about dealing with anxiety. Everything
goes to the mouth to relieve the anxiety from within. In
our adult years, it is best reflected through physical
behaviors such as eating (to either extreme), drinking,
and smoking. We reinforce and camouflage much of
our anxiety through such excessive behaviors. We have
become "experts" at avoiding our pain through various
other means such as sex, television, work, approval,
money, etc.

When I avoided pain, I avoided healing.

Avoiding pain would be the primary cause of my
emotional problems because emotional numbing prevented expression, adjustment, and ultimate healing.
But God wouldn't heal what I continued to avoid. Avoidance behaviors didn't give me permanent relief because
they didn't reach the problem's core. Jesus made no
attempt to avoid the pain of life.

What I didn't know then was that most addictive
behaviors are symptoms of inner conflict. According to
Earl Henslin, "An addiction is anything that consumes
the focus of our attention, distances us from God,
prevents us from facing ourselves, or anything that
hinders us from being emotionally available in our

relationships with God or people."[1] Even our emotions can become addictive, so internal changes must occur if the external changes are going to last. As a false substitute, alcohol prevented me from feeling and experiencing genuine love and intimacy. The alcohol was a symptom of my inability or unwillingness to face the hurt of reality by hanging onto various forms of fantasy. By playing dodge ball between reality and fantasy, I put myself in a sure lose situation. Many people approach the concept of "addiction" with a self-righteous attitude, assuming it doesn't apply to them. But all of us suffer from the most deadly addiction of all—the addiction to self.

Alcoholism can have a genetic link, but much of it, like any other behavior, is learned. It can become an addiction out of control, but it starts and ends with choice. It is sin because it separates us from God. Drinking becomes a formal addiction when willpower alone isn't enough for people to regain control. One should respect the complexities of alcoholism as one does a disease such as cancer. But unlike many diseases, it can be stopped. Overall, Alcoholics Anonymous (AA) has proven to be the best deterrent for alcoholism: there is validity and strength in numbers of people and their experiences. J. B. Phillips said it best when he declared, "You belong to the power you choose to obey."

Prior dysfunctional family life and the unresolved personal trauma of the accident were the roots of my alcohol problem. In one sense, my father was still an emotionally-wounded child seeking love and approval. He learned to depend on the cheap and shallow substitute of alcohol for a sense of power or control over his hurt. Eventually he became enslaved to the substitute and went full circle, once again becoming powerless and completely out of control. The first step in AA's twelve-step-recovery program is to admit to being powerless over alcohol. But the illusion my father, and to a certain extent myself, had was that we were still in control.

The only power anyone has is the power to admit he or she is powerless. Just hours before his death, Jesus chose to become powerless. In the garden, He chose to drink the cup of redemptive and creative suffering. Jesus chose a path leading into the teeth of suffering (John 10:17-18).

Our brokenness and powerlessness are the table setters for His power. The same power that raised Christ from the dead could have been mine for the taking. Christ accepted weakness and powerlessness to become the power of God for us. Because He chose to become a slave, He can now proclaim release to the captives and freedom for those in bondage. Donald Bloesch states that the prison has been stormed, and its gates have been opened, but unless we have the courage to leave our prison cells and move forward into the light of freedom, we are still unredeemed.

My drinking behavior allowed me to erroneously pinpoint something concrete for my miserable condition. "I have a drinking problem" felt less personal and threatening, as compared to the spiritual problem of not having my sins forgiven. The religious realm was completely foreign to me, and the emotional pain just became stronger as I continued to avoid it. Denial is the process by which our unconscious resists change. In denial, we find no objective truth. Our objectivity slowly erodes through various forms of gradual deceptiveness. Denial is merely an inaccurate appraisal of reality. As John Drakeford puts it, "Rationalization has been called the counterfeit of reason."

As his threshold of tolerance increased over the years, my father didn't necessarily drink to get drunk, but more frightening, he drank to feel normal. Spiritually, normal isn't something we should settle for. Normal is estrangement from God. In addition, my father's poor impulse control and low frustration tolerance level were primary ingredients for disaster. He had a vast storehouse of anger, often subtly smoldering just below his conscious awareness.

Many people have no idea how much internal change is needed to break an addiction. As Ted Roberts explains, "This depth of change doesn't come in a moment. It usually takes three to five years to go through the process, with God working miracles every step of the way. The goal isn't just to get the noose off the soul, but to become someone who is experiencing all that God has for him."[2] Alcoholism does not discriminate in levels of education, income, age, or gender. It is an equal opportunity dysfunction.

Alcohol had been an ugly, gaping wound within my family for years. All family members were repeatedly traumatized by the timeless drunken rages of my father, some involving shotguns and rifles. On several occasions, I ran out of our house screaming at the top of my lungs to find anyone who could help. Other times, I ran to the backyard and hid behind the biggest tree I could find. My worst childhood memory was at the age of nine, when my father attempted to strangle my mother right in front of me. If I hadn't run to get help from my two older sisters, there is no doubt he would have killed her that night. These terrifying experiences were simply too much for a child to see. Children don't have the coping skills for such traumatic events. I learned to tolerate abuse as a means of getting my father's love and discovered I couldn't get one without the other.

Trauma is an agent of force that knots our emotions. Any person who witnesses violence is also a victim of violence. But in accordance with the dynamics of a dysfunctional family, any help would threaten the system. And no one in our family would receive any formal treatment. No outsiders were to invade. We didn't get better; we stayed the same—frozen in fear. The goal was balance, not better. We dared not to leave the family or we would become "selfish or disloyal." All family members became very loyal, but our loyalty was to secrecy, shame, and terror. A tremendous amount of energy was used to maintain the massive cover-up. With so much focus on my father and his drinking, it was easy to feel empty or invisible. Initially, ignorance convinced me that every household worked in the same fashion. Friction fueled our dysfunctional family. Alice Miller says, "It is not the traumas we suffer in childhood which makes us emotionally ill but the inability to express the trauma."

Although my father didn't drink the last seven years of his life, the physical consequences of the alcoholism (cirrhosis of the liver and brain dementia) claimed his earthly life at the age of 59. Thankfully, he had finally defeated all his childhood demons years before when he gave his life to Christ. His demons were eventually transformed into angels through the love of Christ. In essence, he tried to outrun his abusive childhood through alcohol. But it would be a race he would lose. He did win his ultimate race through Christ, and I am very proud of him. Alcohol will never deliver what we need.

My emotional immaturity was reflected in impulsive, knee-jerk decisions or behavior primarily based in emotion. In alcoholic-oppressive atmospheres, one is not allowed to feel, change, or grow. I couldn't express the full gamut of my feelings because it was not tolerated. Boundaries and limits were blurred or nonexistent. In some instances, I had to be the male "parent" in the home to replace my alcoholic father. Therefore, I was never consistently allowed to be a child. I was a parent by default, but without the necessary maturity or coping skills. Another dynamic of the alcoholic home was revealed. A child cannot feel, but he is also unable to play.

My emotional growth was thwarted through the brutality of fear and intimidation. Children often unconsciously feel they are responsible for their parent's drinking, and as adults, they often have an over-developed or distorted sense of responsibility. In our family, feelings were actually more disciplined than our behavior. So, many of my emotions were just below the surface wanting to burst out simultaneously. These emotions were both healthy and painful. Yet I didn't know how to express them in an appropriate way because I didn't have the experience to do so. By the time of the accident, I was chronologically twenty years old, but because of the alcoholic background, I would estimate my emotional age to be about twelve years of age.

- 4 -

THE RECOVERING JOURNEY
SPUTTERS

"The Lord is close to the brokenhearted and
saves those who are crushed in spirit."
Psalm 34:18

Due to the advice of friends and the genuine positive impression the pastor had made on our family, we
began to attend church regularly. Until this tragic event,
attending church had never been a consistent way of life
for us. We were more influenced by the inconsistency
and trauma of alcohol. For example, I can remember
going to Easter sunrise service with my drunken father
who had not slept off the alcohol from the night before.
The numerous glares were humiliating.

A few months after the accident, desperation started
to set in. I had tried everything in my attempt to cope,
with the exception of having a personal relationship
with God. I had a limited knowledge of God but no
active relationship with Him. Even well before the

accident, there had been a spiritual void in my life. I had become more conscious of the void, realizing it had grown to the size of a large canyon. In the aftermath of the tragedy, God was working diligently behind the scenes to illustrate the immense size and depth of the void. He was showing me that it could never be filled by any earthly attachments. The emphasis was probably needed to get and maintain my attention. Although I dared not tell anyone, in the back of my mind I felt "Christmas Day" was a message from God such as: "This is a horrible situation, but I am with you." Hanging on to "Christmas Day" was a way to sense His Presence; but more importantly, to sense His desire just to hold and love me.

Tragic Lightning Again

Even more shocking news followed the accident. Only nine months after Tina's death, her 15-year-old sister and a companion died in another car accident while walking along a highway on the other side of town. I will never understand the magnitude of pain and loss Tina's mother and remaining family members have experienced. How do you lose so much and continue to move forward? Surely, this was beyond the scope to expect anyone to bear. These cruel circumstances were certainly the epitome of unfairness and injustice. God must be showing His level of selfishness in the most abhorrent way. In my mind, tragedy and heartache had been brutally redefined. The words of the psalmist saying, "The troubles of my heart have multiplied; free me from my anguish" (Psalm 25:17), echoed my own feelings.

Tina's sister's death brought a lot of unresolved feelings back to the surface. My careless behavior contributed to Tina's family's overall grief; but I also feared my part could push one of her family members over the edge. I felt helpless when I thought of her family as they continued to be bombarded by tragic deaths. Two of the three deaths had nothing to do with me, but I still felt responsible in the totality of their overwhelming grief. I wanted to feel better by being burdened with more of their grief.

Two months later I came home from college for Thanksgiving weekend feeling completely lost. On Saturday night, I drove up to a fender bender, and I remember a man stepping out of one of the cars. He was in a daze and slightly bleeding as he walked right past me. A rush of indescribable energy hit me like a refreshing, cleansing ocean wave. God's Spirit was speaking to me again. It was high time to walk away from the death of chaotic sin and toward my Heavenly Father. I never saw the man again, but I do know he represented Christ.

In joyful tears of triumph, I drove to the home of my associate pastor, Jeff Spicer, and told him of my decision. We walked to a back room and got on our knees to pray, and I became a Christian. The next morning, with a spirit of growing anticipation and excitement, I publicly accepted Jesus Christ as my Savior. When I walked up to the altar, I was startled and yet amazed to see how many people in the church were crying with me.

Although my faith was genuine and sincere, due to my spiritual immaturity, I misunderstood my decision. What I naively expected was a form of magic that would make me feel better instantly. No lightning bolts, thunder, or profound audible voices were heard that morning or any day thereafter. I wish it could be that easy. The illusion was just a cruel hoax I had pulled on myself. My soul received forgiveness for my sins and the gift of eternal life, but my heart continued to feel burdened and guilty. I didn't understand that salvation for the deliverance from the power and effects of sin could have little or no immediate impact on my current emotional state. Salvation represents the beginning of liberation from ignorance and illusion; we usually find the realization of God's supremacy after a long journey of searching. Ingrained behavioral and cognitive patterns can take a great deal of time to correct in the process of our transformation. We are saved and we are new creatures, but we are still prone to old habits. As important as breaking old behavioral habits was, it was harder still for me to begin creating new spiritual ones.

By adamantly refusing to forgive myself, God's gentle stream of grace was dammed from reaching me. In spite of my salvation, I became engrossed in a mutiny from within by choosing to hang on tight to the past, rather than reaching forward to experience the fullness of God's grace. I got caught up in the awe and wonder of my particular valley by emphasizing the abyss rather than the size, uniqueness, and love of God. I did not adhere to the words of Paul, "Brothers, I do not consider myself yet to have taken hold of it. But one thing I do: Forgetting what is behind and straining toward what is ahead" (Philippians 3:13).

Reaching forward was frightening to me. I was afraid of what I was putting my heart and hands into. It reminded me of Paul Tournier's description of a failing trapeze artist; too frozen in fear to reach forward for the coming baton and too frozen to let go of the other. I continued to dangle back and forth, repeating the same old, conforming, mundane routine. A desolate rut became my model of life, both emotionally and physically.

Hanging onto the adversity was becoming more harmful than the adversity itself, because it was creating boulders of emotional baggage. What inner payoffs could there be by hanging on? Was I willing to give them up in order to get healthy? Unknowingly, my self-imposed victimization became the root of my identity as the trauma fused with my sense of self. I didn't know who I was without the trauma. I wanted to let go, but at the same time, I couldn't or wouldn't let go.

The road to my recovery would involve more suffering. The thought of recovery and its inevitable anguish was too much for me. I, not fully believing and accepting God's resources, certainly did not want any more heartache, even in the "religious" realm. A broken heart heals slowly, and it may not be prepared to be handled too soon. Grace and forgiveness were relatively new concepts to me, and I simply did not understand all of their dynamics. Ignorance and indifference are very powerful weapons of self-destruction. I was too impulsive to agree to gradual change, and a layer-by-layer recovery process had no appeal. I wanted the fix to be as quick as the adversity. Quick-fix solutions can actually overlook the power of God.

Recovery is the complicated process of restoring a person to a quality state of being and usefulness. Initially, it was my attempt to reclaim what I had lost. But I needed to recover without regaining what was now gone. Hopefully, the healing process would give me many tangibles I never had before, making me stronger for the future and for the passing down of my own legacy. Recovery is an ongoing passage to freedom.

But I remained preoccupied and self-absorbed with my issues, which reinforced my deepening bewilderment. My emotional problems were due to a spiritual conflict: specifically, the lack of self-forgiveness. Yet when I tried to forgive myself, I used only my feeble power and strength. I had not learned what the Lord said to Zechariah, "Not by might nor by power, but by my Spirit" (Zechariah 4:6).

I attached forgiveness to performance, making it conditional and an impossible feat to achieve, or better yet, to simply receive. Performance was just an offspring of self-righteousness, and a treadmill could have easily become my latest altar. It was one thing to stay on the treadmill to receive many things, but I remained fearful of ever getting off. My "What can I do?" mentality needed to change to "What has already been done for me?"

Although I had asked Christ into my heart, when I needed Him the most, I turned my back on Him. This caused the anger, guilt, and shame to have no functional outlets through which to be expressed or resolved. I didn't realize it took more mental energy to suppress my feelings than to express them. When I became "too busy" suppressing painful feelings, I missed experiencing all the enjoyable ones, too.

Over the next several months, I took three medical withdrawals from college and admitted myself into local hospitals for treatment of depression. Each time I tried to go back to school, I would feel the overwhelming need to withdraw within just a few days. The act of withdrawing was about the only thing I could control. I had no ability to concentrate, and I felt increasingly isolated and detached through irrational thinking and fear. As an example, I felt that all of my college friends were leaving me behind as they continued in their studies. The onslaught of guilt continued.

Prayer, the Ultimate Dialogue

"Cast your cares on the Lord and he will sustain you."

Psalm 55:22

Prayer is God's loving invitation to have an intimate relationship with Him. But my inexperience in the Christian way of life became quite evident. I felt my prayers were unanswered, so I became further discouraged and stopped praying. Prayers need the components of trust, humility, and perseverance, everything mine lacked. My perceived needs were unknowingly subtle, selfish demands, which were not within the will of God. God's means of handling this particular situation was not on my terms or what I had imagined. His answer(s) is what I needed, but what I needed was the furthest thing from my mind. Prayers were not answered in my way, and God's timeline or cosmic clock seemed inconvenient and troublesome to my schedule. Waiting is an essential form of spiritual discipline, and I didn't realize that God's timing would be ultimately right for me. The Psalmist David said, "I wait for the Lord, my soul waits, and in his word I put my hope. My soul waits for the Lord more than watchmen wait for the morning...." (Psalm 130:5-6).

There is no such thing as unanswered prayer (I John 5:14). John Wesley once said all God does is answer prayer. The answer is either yes, no, or wait. His answer(s) would always be in my best interest, but I needed to learn it may not always be within my best reason. I would pray for the wrong things (what I wanted) rather than what I needed (what God wanted me to have). Just as in good, solid parenting, if God gave his children everything they wanted and nothing they needed, they would eventually lose respect for Him. "No" does not mean God didn't answer. It was just an answer I didn't want to hear. I needed to remember that God is as great when He denies my prayer requests as when He grants them. The bounty of prayer is in a God who hears it.

My prayers aren't necessarily answered just because I earnestly believe God can deliver, but because God wills it that way, for at least the time being. So my prayer life would need to be based on the realization that God knows more about life than I do. Genuine prayer and any effective results would depend on my ability to acknowledge the depths of my own helplessness. Prayer would become my never-ending lifeline to God. Often prayer is unintentionally demeaned, especially in times of adversity because it is used as a means of last resort, such as "All that is left to do is just pray," rather than prayer being our first and foremost response.

God's third response of answering prayers often required more than I was willing to give, which included patience most of all. Impatience is often a sign of hidden anger, inner conflict, and the frustration of being out of control. Patience is a work-in-progress for many people, including myself. I often demanded that God do something now, without realizing the very difficult work He and I had yet to do together.

"A man's wisdom gives him patience..."

Proverbs 19:11

Anger

Depression was fueled by repressed anger turned inward. Depressed people are often very angry at someone or something, including themselves, although they may not be aware of it. I was angry at myself, at God, and at Tina. God was not threatened by my anger toward Him. He understood my context. Anger, like any other emotion, is designed to be good. For example, when Jesus went into the temple, He illustrated righteous anger by overturning the tables, and not the people, because of their inappropriate behavior (John 2:15).

Indignation stresses righteous anger at what one considers unfair or shameful. In dealing with anger, I needed to be more assertive with my feelings in order to prevent hostility and aggression. Swallowing anger over an extended period of time only ensured a later volcanic eruption. I had swallowed a lifetime's worth but had no idea.

When we assert our feelings, we state them in a positive way without regard for approval. Thus, we demonstrate the existence of the feelings. Assertiveness implies openness and conviction. If we are unable or unwilling to assert our feelings, we cannot expect anyone to respect them. Assertiveness is a form of respect for our own feelings and selves. For most of my adolescence and young adult years, I was shy and withdrawn and was very poor at assertiveness. At home I had learned to speak only when spoken to. I walked on eggshells to avoid a confrontation with my father.

As a result I became hostile, probably because I didn't talk about the problem. Hostility, on the other hand, is a by-product of a lack of assertiveness. It is conflict (internal or external), opposition, or resistance in thought(s) or principle. My own mind became a very hostile confine. The antagonism was directed toward others but even more so toward myself. Aggression, on the other hand, is an over-compensation intended to dominate or master others through combative behavior. It is marked by a driving, forceful energy, an energy not previously used through assertiveness. Escalation of my inner anger was a direct correlation of how poorly I originally asserted my feelings. Romans 8: 6-7 says: "The mind of sinful man is death, but the mind controlled by the Spirit is life and peace; the sinful mind is hostile to God."

- 5 -

THE NEED FOR GOD'S POWER

"and his incomparably great power for us who believe. That power is like the working of his mighty strength."

Ephesians 1:19

During my hospitalizations, I underwent the traditional individual and group therapies and was given a large array of medications. For years I was compliant with taking prescribed medication. In the long run, however, it was not what made a significant impact on my emotional problems. Forgiveness was not a chemical issue; it was a spiritual dilemma based upon my poor choices. Medication cannot give anyone forgiveness. Medication can be a valued resource where God works through technology, but it shouldn't be viewed as a panacea. Most anti-depressant medication is designed as a supplement to help stabilize our mood while we resolve emotional issues. Many people use medication as a remedy for all ills. Medication can even lower our motivation to resolve issues by masking some of the painful, yet healthy, consequences of our behavior or thinking. We also have a tendency to settle because we are feeling better.

The main reason medication does not work is that people do not follow the directions. A person starts to feel better and then decides he no longer needs the medication, or one does not feel any improvement and out of frustration, stops taking it. Although a person may not feel relief, he could actually feel a great deal worse without the medication. It may have taken months or even years to become clinically depressed. It is unreasonable to think a few days or weeks of medication will necessarily reverse a chemical imbalance. Major depression usually takes time on both ends to fully manifest itself through its symptoms and its eventual treatment and cure(s). Everyone is unique. For many, swallowing a pill is the most spiritual thing they can do. But God's healing requires much more than just feeling better, since feelings alone don't resolve issues. I had to get well below the glossy finish in order to be healed.

During one of my hospitalizations, I met a male nurse, John, who years before had experienced a severe trauma when his wife and three children were killed in a car accident. He, too, had experienced major depression, which required hospitalization. I asked him what the turning point had been for him. He replied it was the moment he began realizing "that most people don't give a ——." I immediately wrote his comments off as someone who was still understandably bitter and resentful. But the more I thought about it, the clearer his point became. At the time, John provided an understanding of Christ to me. My unrealistic expectations of faith and myself had spread to others. Little did I realize how people (certainly including myself) become so wrapped up in their individual lives. Many people are addicted to rushing and are often too consumed with their own issues to notice or care. I had developed tunnel vision with no peripheral awareness by focusing only on what was before me: creating an out-of-sight and out-of-thought mentality. I also needed to focus on others' feelings, thoughts, and perspectives, too. My feelings were not the center of the universe, and there have been other tragic car accidents.

John's words began to help me detach and disengage from what I perceived as many people not being able to understand. I stopped expecting them to. How could they possibly understand in the first place? The accident wasn't to be understood. Without realizing it, I wanted the power to bring others into my misery. Yet by making my expectations of them more reasonable, I was able to begin to take a great deal of pressure off myself. Our rapid-fire and fast-paced culture simply does not nurture sensitivity. At the same time, I needed to acquire some tough skin.

"Therefore put on the full armor of God, so that when the day of evil comes, you may be able to stand your ground, and after you have done everything, to stand."

Ephesians 6:13

John and a psychiatric social worker by the name of Lois, a survivor of the German concentration camps, gave me some powerful insights on the plight of human tragedy. They had my utmost respect, but I didn't find the peace they had come to know. I continued to think: My situation is different. In spite of their seasoned help and expertise, I felt no positive results.

The psychiatrists recommended two sets of ECT (electro-convulsive shock therapy). Initially, I was afraid of these treatments, but I was more scared of living the way that I had been. This medical option is usually recommended only after every other avenue of treatment for depression has been exhausted. When people think of ECT, many may recall the terrifying image of Jack Nicholson in *One Flew Over the Cuckoo's Nest*. The movie reflected Hollywood's version and not reality. There is no doubt ECT can be an effective procedure and a crucial turning point in the treatment of major depression. Experts are still uncertain as to how or why it works. It is generally believed that ECT acts by temporarily altering some of the brain's electrochemical processes.

One of the frequent side effects is short-term memory loss, especially in and around the time of treatments. But being so depressed after all other treatment has been exhausted, many people figure some memory loss during the worst time of their lives will be a reasonable sacrifice to make. That was certainly my rationale, but the treatments brought only temporary improvement. An internal gnawing kept telling me there was a "peace" missing. Similar to medication, ECT cannot supply forgiveness. I needed a power that technology could not give.

I felt I had a right to suffer. Suffering, combined with self-pity and an ongoing resentment of myself, became barriers to God's grace. In essence, I fell in love with my sorrow by drawing an imaginary circle around myself and my circumstances. Self-pity resulted from focusing on myself rather than on God. Melancholy and hopelessness eventually overwhelmed me, and I saw no reason to go on with life. What was the point? I simply couldn't find any meaning within the suffering.

I chose not to be vulnerable to God's love and grace because vulnerability scared me; the thought of letting my guard down and being transparent to Him frightened me. People in authority had often hurt and disappointed me by giving mixed messages for much of my life.

Mistrust had been bred from my alcoholic father. Without realizing it, I had transferred that mistrust to my Heavenly Father, my ultimate authority figure.

How we view and respond to authority figures is one of the most important aspects in describing our relationship with Christ. In Christ, the call to authority is the call to self-sacrifice. Because of unresolved authority issues, I was more inclined to be in a self-preservation mode, which directly conflicted with my need to self-sacrifice. Authority should be a warm and nurturing word, but because of my past experiences, it was an empty, distant, and fearful word. Fear easily outweighed the dynamics of my faith. Therefore, I began to take comfort in the rut and monotony of misery. A solitary ditch offered many fringe benefits. It had become comfortable, known, nonconfrontational, and posed little or no risk. In this sense, there was no real incentive to change. Rather than receiving His forgiveness, I chose my standards. Rather than experiencing His grace, I chose my guilt. I had given my guilt more power than His blood.

I was getting to the point where I had convinced myself I had tried everything, even religion. Religion, (the "r" word) as I knew it at the time, became just another major disappointment. I tried God only after everything else had failed. Trust was still in short supply. "Religion" was checked off my "to do" list in trying to cope with what had occurred. Faith was just a mere option on my crowded menu of coping behaviors.

Faith should be based on a personal relationship and a deep sense of connectedness, not a mere set of rules. Rules can be a cheap substitute for an intimate relationship, especially if a person does not know how to have a relationship or fears having one. As with basic parenting skills, rules without relationship will only result in rebellion. I was now in the middle of an all out rebellion.

Suicide

Suicide became my next option. I actually felt entitled to it because all of my previous and well-meaning efforts had miserably failed. This wasn't about any sense of attention or a crying out for help. I wanted to die. I was convinced that life was not worth living. I had even written a suicide note to my parents.

In a sense of frustrated desperation, one night I drove to the accident site. The same stars that had not protected us the night of the accident were out and were watching me again as I defiantly swallowed an assortment of pills. But rather than a sense of peace, I felt an intense fear after swallowing the pills. God's Spirit was telling me to get help. Intensity was something I could respond to, and I was able to thwart my own attempt with the help of a policeman on patrol who "just happened" to be driving by. Once in the hospital, it felt like the ultimate defeat had occurred. I couldn't even get suicide right. To add more insult to injury, hospital cameras were constantly watching me. Paranoia had now joined the cast of characters in the ensemble of my irrational thinking.

The goal in many suicide attempts isn't necessarily death, but a means to end a person's emotional agony. I had convinced myself the only way to end the anguish was to end my life. I was wrong. Many people think of suicide in a fleeting manner. For the numerous heartaches people have to experience, it is an understandable thought. As Martin Luther put it, "We cannot prevent the birds from flying over our head, but we can prevent them from building their nests in our hair." It has been said that suicide is a long-term (eternal) solution for a short-term problem. But what about the person who has struggled for years with severe bouts of depression?

Suicide is the most severe, distorted, and deceptive form of self-criticism, self-hatred, and, yes, selfishness. Sometimes, it may be one's last attempt to control a situation or person. It is also a sin against those who are left behind, because survivors of suicide will have a very tumultuous journey ahead. Because they are so emotionally overwhelmed, people who commit (or attempt) suicide have no idea how much they hurt their loved ones left behind. Their death may leave a haunting impact for generations to come.

Depression can be a silent killer. Although depression can be a consequence of a conflicting lifestyle or poor choices, it is in no way a strict "measure" of one's faith. Depression and other forms of mental illness may have nothing to do with the depth of one's faith or character. To imply otherwise is ignorance.

In reference to the eternal consequences of suicide, we have a fair, loving, merciful and understanding God. Over time, major depression causes our thinking to become irrational. One could argue that if a person were a true believer they wouldn't be thinking of suicide as an option. But it's not that cut and dried. Major depression alters everything. The general irrationality of suicide can indeed be a result of distorted thinking and/or chemical imbalances.

In my opinion, for Christians, the suicidal act (self-condemnation) will not be met with God's condemnation. God certainly forgives the sin of murder. Although suicide is a form of rejection of hope in Christ, what follows is between God, the individual, and the mitigating circumstances. Suicide is certainly a sin, but it is not a sin that can't and won't be forgiven. His grace will be evidenced at our death as it was at our birth.

Accordingly, people should not be judged strictly on the means of their death, but rather on the nature of their life.

Within the social principles of the United Methodist Church we find: "A Christian perspective on suicide begins with an affirmation of faith that nothing, including suicide, separates us from the love of God." This statement is rooted in the following verses:

> "For I am convinced that neither death nor life, neither angels nor demons, neither the present nor the future, nor any powers, neither height nor depth, nor anything else in all creation, will be able to separate us from the love of God that is in Christ Jesus our Lord."
>
> Romans 8:38-39

There is no Scripture regarding suicide as an unforgivable sin. To be fair, some could argue that not all suicide attempts are necessarily irrational. Many people prefer to die rather than to be a continuing emotional and financial burden to their families. There can always be debate over what is and isn't rational. There are many complicated variables involved in examining the motivation for suicide where one may be trying to escape responsibility or consequences. One word of caution: we need to be very careful not to give "permission" to commit suicide by emphasizing that it can be forgiven or by taking the subject too lightly. Always contact a mental health professional regarding any suspicion of a potential suicide attempt. It is a false assumption that we are putting suggestive impressions into one's mind by talking about it.

Faith should be based on facts and not on feelings and that should work both ways. I needed to accept by faith the facts of what God had said about me. It may have been tougher to do because of my extremely affective make-up. The facts of my faith would need to come forward and give me a stronger foundation. Feelings cannot always be trusted; they sway up and down, but facts remain steadfast. Feelings should never be the gauge by which I measure the eternal truths of God.

Because of my previous treatment and the general lack of any sustained improvement, I was voluntarily admitted to the state mental hospital in Chattahoochee, Florida, for an indefinite stay. The psychiatrists had run out of options, too. I was willing to do anything to lift the dense and dreadful emotional fog. No functional or dysfunctional treatments had worked, and life was passing me by. Two years had now passed since the accident.

Because the hospital was a state facility and I was currently a patient at a local hospital, I had to take the longest and loneliest trip of my life. During the two-hour drive in the back of a police cruiser, I was frightened every moment, literally feeling like a caged common criminal. In the midst of the trip, I realized my biggest emotional adversaries to overcome were guilt and shame. Like so many emotions, I didn't have a thorough understanding of their divine function. To deal effectively with the guilt and shame, I would have to discover the profound meanings of God's grace and forgiveness. Although I had no earthly idea, I was about to embark on a deeper spiritual journey. The extraordinary setting of a state hospital would allow me the time and space necessary to become aware of, and to explore and express such feelings and concepts.

"...in order that they may know the mystery of God, namely, Christ in whom are hidden all the treasures of wisdom and knowledge."
Colossians 2:2-3

- 6 -

BREAKING FREE FROM THE BONDAGE OF GUILT

"Let us draw near to God with a sincere heart in full assurance of faith, having our hearts sprinkled to cleanse us from a guilty conscience and having our bodies washed with pure water."

Hebrews 10:22

Upon being processed into the hospital, I was assigned to "Unit 1." This unit included many people suffering from severe emotional trauma. I had an intense fear of being locked behind closed doors, and the constant incoherent screaming by some of the patients wore on my nerves. Members of the hospital staff often forcefully subdued patients. Compared to these people, many actively psychotic, I had a strong sense of feeling out of place. Many times I was afraid to take a shower.

In a few weeks, I was transferred to "Unit 26" and earned the privilege to walk the grounds. On that first day, I felt an immediate tug toward the chapel. The tug was undoubtedly God's Spirit. Within the chapel, a small library soon became my refuge in the midst of such mental anguish. I started to read everything I could get my eyes on and began to regularly listen to Christian music for the first time in my faith walk. Prayer, books, and music began to add new dimensions to my life. Reading led me into an unknown world, and it would help me further comprehend the specific dynamics of guilt, shame, grace, and forgiveness. The Bible is God's voice speaking to us. But not until I seriously started to read it was I convinced it was written just for me.

> "Your word, O Lord, is eternal; it stands firm in the heavens."
>
> Psalm 119:89

It must be noted here that, although reading in the hospital's chapel was clearly an enriching experience and a spiritual spark for me, I learned most of the academic knowledge of psychology in my formal training to be a therapist many years later. Thus, the term "reading" may incorporate many years of an evolving knowledge base.

Ground Zero

When beginning to read the Bible, I thought specifically of how it related to my current situation and related trauma. In trying to understand guilt as a whole, I was able to discover many important aspects. The Bible begins with a detailed description of guilt. God wanted us to understand the meaning of guilt from the beginning. Almost every emotional disturbance within our human experience can be traced to the fall of man in the garden. Guilt and shame were first manifested the moment Adam and Eve ate the forbidden fruit. They wanted all the answers to life before gaining knowledge through experience. Because of their sin, God set in motion His incredible master plan of redemption through grace and forgiveness. With His echoing words "Where are you?" (Genesis 3:9), God began an all-out mission for the human heart. And the plan wasn't finished until Christ said so on the cross.

Prohibiting the first couple from eating the forbidden fruit tells us God never intended for man to experience the maladjustment of guilt. Adam and Eve's guilt was very intense because they were not created to deal with it. Guilt was a by-product of their disobedience. Wewer Keohane candidly states, "The problem with Adam and Eve wasn't the apple in the tree, but it was the 'pair' on the ground." But God developed a biblical solution for guilt through the principle(s) of union, adoption, and deliverance with Christ. Guilt and shame (like all sin and blessings) have passed through the generations from Adam and Eve.

Because of Satan's alluring temptation(s) and Adam and Eve's sin, we became destined for Hell. Accusation is Satan's sly strategy to get us to give up on God and condemn ourselves. He manipulates our guilt as part of a powerful arsenal to get us to focus on ourselves rather than on God. E. Stanley Jones writes, "When Satan attacks you, command him in the name of Jesus to bend his neck. On the back of it you'll find there's a nail-scarred footprint."

Guilt means feeling bad for something we have or haven't done. Shame means feeling bad for who we are. I had a huge emotional investment in both markets. Guilt was like a mocking voice continually whispering to me that I had made the biggest mistake a person could make and that I was a poor excuse for a human being. The content of the message was only outweighed by its ceaseless nature. I also feared the dread and horror of another episode of thinking and reliving every meticulous detail of that terrifying night. These obsessive, powerful thoughts completely drained my energy. Everything else in life came to an abrupt standstill as I continued to ruminate in the reruns.

Dr. James Dobson writes, "At the peak of intensity, self-condemnation gnaws on the conscious mind by day and invades our dreams by night. Since the voice of conscience speaks from inside the human mind, we cannot escape its unrelenting abuse for our mistakes, failures and sins."[1] One of my persistent nightmares was the recreating of the accident scene the instant before impact. The car headlights had taken dead aim for the lower trunk of the tree, and we were at the point of no return, literally one second from impending disaster. But now I was observing the car from behind and would begin to yell frantically, "Stop, Stop!" to get anyone's attention, but no one would ever hear me.

Forms of Guilt

Guilt that produces a constructive sorrow is called righteous or true guilt. This form of guilt has a divine purpose. A righteous sense of guilt is actually a gift from God. And, yes, guilt is good. Without it, no one would be motivated to repentance. The Bible tells us guilt is our natural condition, for we are all guilty in the sight of God. Godly sorrow prompts a positive and lasting change.

I learned through my reading that psychological or false guilt, on the other hand, is a feeling only. It consists of feelings of culpability for real or imagined offenses or from a sense of inadequacy. These feelings are always destructive and cause spiritual deprivation, poor mental health, and self-inflicted misery. It is a corrosive and acidic guilt born in sin or evil that no human can escape on his own strength. According to Lucy Freeman and Herbert Strean, "The ways we choose to avoid guilt are far more dangerous than facing guilt itself."

The Bible never encourages believers in Jesus Christ to accept psychological guilt, nor are Christians commanded to have a fear of punishment, a sense of worthlessness, or a feeling of rejection. There are no translations of the word "guilt" referring to the feeling of guilt. Instead, the Scriptures interpret it as meaning "to be liable to judgment," "to be guilty of an offense," or "to owe or be indebted to." These are all states of being.

When guilt began to consume me, I conned myself into thinking that if I had to live, it would be in a wretched condition. I rationalized that I didn't deserve to get better. I felt worthy of the guilt and began to embrace it. The savage and vicious self-perpetuating guilt cycle began to snowball—guilt for what had occurred and guilt for daring to feel better. This wasn't a righteous sense of guilt from God, but a manufactured (psychological) guilt I created and even nursed. An overactive and irrational conscience, rooted to some degree in my dysfunctional past, had formed. In short, guilt became my God. Charles Spurgeon describes the encompassing power of guilt when he states, "A thorn in the flesh is nothing in comparison to a thorn in the conscience."

My guilt was also revealed in anger. I was often more irritable, felt constantly on edge, and seemed to have a constant inner sense of combativeness. Guilt was a signal that something was wrong, which created an internal tension or threat of rejection. Anger and hostility were often used as coping mechanisms in fighting the perceived rejection. Yielding to self-pity, depression, and rebellion was a waste of sorrow. All were distinct forms of anger. The most angry people are the most hurt people, but they are also the most immature, specifically in how well they manage their anger. Their anger is what actually manages them and their relationships. Rage hides the emptiness and hurt of their hearts. Other than guilt and shame, the emotion I needed most to come to terms with was anger.

In my reading, I learned to reason that if I became enslaved to bitterness, I would be wasting what God intended for spiritual growth. Bitterness is no more than a tightly knit circle of self-centered rage. Maurice Nesbitt writes, "Because of unresolved anger, we are also in danger of becoming prisoners of the past entombed in a pillar of emotional and spiritual salt."[2] Bitterness was a mental venom that would only hurt me. As long as I had unresolved anger, someone or something else had controlling interest of my life. And when God was not the master of my life, I had a bigger need for my own controlling behaviors. Controlling behaviors ultimately lead us to what we fear the most: rejection.

Looking back, in my false sense of guilt, I needed to suffer more in order to try to fulfill my penitence requirements. The heartache and agony intensified because I didn't realize I was the source of this spirit-crushing torment. I didn't trust God's love and forgiveness to wipe away guilt and liberate me to live in Christ and in His image. My guilt demanded more of a price. Hell had become the state of my mind. As T.S. Eliot says, "Hell is oneself." Treading water quickly became too tiresome, and I started to drown in a makeshift pool of guilt and shame with no known life preserver.

I assumed the guilt would sever me from God forever. Ironically, it would be the guilt that would eventually connect me to Him. But through my previous misunderstanding and misapplication of faith as a whole, I tended to maximize the guilt and minimize God and His resources. Within the confines of my childish playground, my self-made see-saw between God and guilt became perilously tipped in the wrong direction. In fact, my feet rarely left the muck of the ground.

But I soon learned that guilt is not necessarily the power of God's conviction. Conscience is helpful, but it is an imperfect tool often distorted by the internalized values we have learned in our family of origin. Conscience is the sense of moral goodness or blameworthiness of one's own conduct, combined with an obligation to do the right thing. Honesty and directness are the products of a good, sound conscience.

My conscience was too tainted by sin in the sense of being inaccurate, excessive, or too rigid. I needed to be vigilant so my conscience remained my guide, not yet another god. My conscience alone only brought confusion. Rather than trusting my conscience, I had to trust the cross and to subject my conscience to the Word of God.

It dawned on me that the Bible outlines a perfect plan of guilt reduction. It speaks to each aspect of the guilt emotion, and it offers a healthy alternative: a true, righteous sense of guilt. God did not deny or rationalize our guilt away. Rather He faced our guilt on Calvary. He took our guilt upon Himself. Jesus "assumed" the sin for us to show His magnificent grace. He bore what we need not carry (I Peter 2:24).

Although I wasn't aware of it, it was my self-centeredness and lack of trust that prevented me from resolving the guilt. I assumed the throne of guilt, making a pivotal mistake in my struggle to get free and stay free. I failed to allow the truth of Colossians 2:13-14 to permeate my soul. "...God made you alive with Christ.

He forgave us all our sins, having canceled the written code, with its regulations, that was against us and that stood opposed to us; he took it away, nailing it to the cross."

Clearly, Jesus' perfect psychological health derives from the fact of His true and total dependence on God. The Bible affirms that the only true guilt is disobedience to God or any dependence other than on God alone. If we sin or disobey, guilt is a good thing. Guilt is one of the necessities of life. Like any other emotion though, guilt needs to be properly harnessed. Through guilt, God desires the appropriate balance, but I tended to take the guilt and shame to their extremes. By doing so, they lost their functional effectiveness or divine purposes.

My emotions were created to guide my behavior, not dominate it. I realized that guilt and shame can initially inhibit good feelings, but they can also be catalysts that actually help the good feelings develop. There is a sense of duality in all emotions. Guilt can change us for the better or it can become a raging cancer within our soul. In the words of Corrie ten Boom, "Guilt never heals, its purpose is only to lead us to the Healer."

Although I needed guilt for repentance, deliverance did not come so quickly. Likewise, the guilt required time to get a stranglehold on me. Tournier tells us, "Repentance may be reached only after a long struggle and a stormy defense; reached when conviction of sin grows from within and not from without, when it rises from the depths of our own being, from intimate communion with God and from the prompting of the Holy Spirit."[3] Conviction led me to the cleansing of confession. Confession would nurture my relationship with God, and prevent me from paying the costly emotional toll of unconfessed sin. It also would give me a sense of accountability and represented the initial step in mending all of my estranged relationships. In confession(s), old desires were being driven out, while my conscience underwent a spiritual upheaval. When I was convicted in a spiritual dimension, I was convinced of my mistakes, but more importantly, of God's love, grace, and forgiveness. Conviction also works in a dual capacity and creates a healthy sense of balance. John 16:8 states, "When he comes, he will convict the world of guilt in regard to sin and righteousness and judgment."

My identity is one of God's forgiven, adopted, chosen, delivered, and sealed children. You and I are His workmanship. My identity is totally separate from what happened to me and from the defense mechanisms, such as guilt, designed to protect me. As David Seamands puts it, "What happens in us is more important than what happens to us. We are not always able to choose the latter, but we can always choose the former." Righteous guilt was the Spirit eating at my conscience and leading me to a redemptive change. I became conscious of my value only through the experience of God's forgiveness.

The Dynamics of Repression

"Repressions are the power that makes one work against all the avowed and willful intentions. They are strong because they are deep in the vows of the child of the past. The adult is simply unable to will them away."[4]

Myron Madden

God blots out conscious guilt, but He also brought to consciousness my repressed guilt. I learned that repression is an unconscious process by which unacceptable feelings, desires, or events, especially from our childhood, are excluded from consciousness. Repression is not necessarily bad for us. Many people have to repress their feelings in order to survive and cope with trauma. When we repress, we shove feelings down by force. These feelings or events can haunt us in our adult years because unconscious feelings can't tell time. Repression hindered the natural expression of my feelings. Tournier further explains, "Repression of guilt brings a hardening of the heart. Guilt towards oneself is at the same time, a guilt toward God, since it is a refusal to accept oneself as God wishes each of us to be."[5] If I were to process the guilt properly, it would become a valued friend by guiding me to the experience of God's grace.

Anxiety

Guilt and anxiety hindered me from living in the present. While guilt focuses more on the past, anxiety focuses more on the future. I was convinced that I didn't have a future because of the past. Madden says: "Guilt can flow into anxiety and escape recognition of itself. Most of the powerful emotions can be held in until they are recognized in their own name. They can ride piggyback on other emotions. Very few people are able to say simply, 'I am guilty.' It is much less incriminating to admit to anxiety."[6]

I discovered that anxiety, which is generally more broad and vague, often attempts to exteriorize and normalize guilt in some generic form to prevent vulnerability and transparency. In essence, for me the anxiety created a state of spiritual deep freeze. Sometimes, the anxiety was a result of my unconscious spiritual tug of war with God for control. No wonder I was so easily distracted and had lost the ability to concentrate. Anxiety was often exacerbated when I began to fear life more than death. Similarly, I was afraid to be happy because I had learned that the other shoe would soon drop. My skeptic mental filters and negative expectations needed to be destroyed.

Intimacy

Intimacy characterizes one's deepest nature. It represents a very close relationship that has developed over a long period of time through the building of trust. It is the substance at the depth of our soul. Intimacy develops when we share our sorrows, but more importantly, when we share our joys with another person. These feelings are not considered to be threatening in any way. In intimate sharing, we feel accepted just as we are because we are emotional equals.

God desired the same warm and affectionate intimacy with me that He had with His Son. The chief obstacle in creating intimacy with Christ was my own desire for independence. When I chose to live for myself rather than God, I condemned myself to isolation. In addition, the fear of rejection hindered me from being intimate with anyone. Fear caused me to mentally wrestle with myself in knowing what to do. I needed intimacy with God through surrender and vulnerability. But it was virtually impossible to surrender and be vulnerable when I was packing false guilt and shame. They robbed my relationships of intimacy through conditional love and fear. Entrenched guilt created distance and rejected any overtures of caring. My ability or willingness to confide was hampered because I didn't feel good enough about myself to trust anyone.

In our quest for intimacy, we often misuse sex as a shallow substitute. Sex is designed to be a responsive celebration of genuine intimacy, a celebration of two personalities united in love with each other, but more importantly, with our loving God. But when sex has selfish motives, such as sex outside of marriage, we actually become lonelier than we were before. Sex will not make us feel secure, but intimacy will. Solomon used alcohol and sex as a way of medicating his woes rather than confronting them. He had over 700 wives and 300 concubines (I Kings 11:3), but he still could not find intimacy and peace.

Guilt categorically denies intimacy. Although intimacy is an incredible state and experience, I feared it and actually preferred darkness and distance over the light and closeness. I did not want to be identified, much less have my feelings exposed or potentially rejected. Exposure was perceived as too humiliating an event. In one way, I began to identify with Jesus in His nakedness on the cross. Yet I didn't embrace His humble standard. I preferred to be a nobody, readily and fatalistically accepting being lost in the middle of a large indifferent crowd.

Childhood Tapes

In dealing with guilt stemming from years past, my faulty childhood authority programming tapes were very difficult to overcome. The term "can't never did anything" felt like a cruel curse, although my father meant it to be a form of encouragement or motivation. When I finally realized many of the decisions my father made were wrong, I discerned the need to be reparented, to a limited degree, by my Heavenly Father. Remembering the past in an appropriate way helped me reconfigure the present and future with desire and hope. We eventually heal by remembering.

We all come out of childhood wounded because of imperfect parenting. Termites are found in virtually all of our family trees. Because of the inconsistent authority in the past, my repressed feelings were manifested in my early adult years in many compulsive behaviors such as: perfectionism, impatience, and self-indulgence. The compulsiveness was the response to an unyielding tyrant who had become internalized in order to replace my inconsistent father. Appropriate authority implies the granting of power for a specific purpose within specified limits. Emotional scars and scabs developed when the authority figure lost its specific purpose and went beyond its specific limits. In short, authority became abuse once the boundaries were enmeshed, lost, or crossed.

- 7 -

GUILT BENEFITS
OR UNCONSCIOUS PAYOFFS

> "Godly sorrow brings repentance that leads to salvation and leaves no regret, but worldly sorrow brings death."
>
> 2 Corinthians 7:10

Guilt gave me an unconscious pleasure from suffering, a chief characteristic of a self-defeating personality. This type of personality chooses people and situations leading to failure even when better options are clearly available. It also rejects the attempts of others to help and engages in excessive self-sacrifice at the expense of self-esteem. Even following positive experiences, many people respond in a negative way, producing more turmoil. They may even incite or provoke hostile responses, but then feel humiliated and devastated over such responses. They thrive on rejection as a way of confirming their own sense of paranoia and worthlessness. In my case, I felt "better" by punishing myself because I deserved it.

Similarly, guilt-induced depression gave me a sense of security. Under stress, many people unconsciously retreat into depression. Depression can provide a false sense of safety in many subtle forms, while we remain blind to the steep cliff just one step to our right. My depression "ditch" provided a sense of safety, as opposed to driving on the dangerous highway itself.

Guilt also gave me an "illusion of control." Many people would rather believe certain events in their lives are a result of their own mistakes, rather than those caused by chance or other circumstances. Elaine Pagels tells us that we have tendency to accept personal blame for suffering. Many people would rather feel guilty than helpless. If the cause of the situation is considered moral rather than natural, we often persuade ourselves we can control it. Guilt is the price to be paid for the illusion of control over nature, but many people have seemed more than willing to pay it.

By owning the guilt, it gave me an unconscious sense of pride and control. If I were to let go of it, I would lose ownership. On an unconscious level, I did not want to cope with any more loss. I had to hold onto something... Clinging to the guilt, regardless of the circumstances, met several needs. Now I had both a companion and a (false) sense of control, where previously I had neither. In addition, I wouldn't forgive myself because I felt it wouldn't honor the depth of my wrongdoing.

Guilt also gave me an increased sense of connectedness to everyone in the car. I didn't want to release any more passengers; I had already lost one. I also had to seek and receive a pardon on God's terms rather than my own. I assumed the need for punishment, but through countless hours of counseling and reading at the hospital, I became aware of an unconscious passive submission to the illness and my general unwillingness to even consider the possibility of recovery. In other words, I was justifying the guilt rather than trying to be freed from it. Feeling guilty became just another entitled form of self-indulgence.

Idolatry

> "From the rest he makes a god, his idol; he bows down to it and worships. He prays to it and says, 'Save me; you are my god.'"
>
> Isaiah 44:17

Clinging to my guilt became a form of idolatry. The Apostle Paul suggests suffering in the world at the hands of human injustice can be reduced to the ultimate source of idolatry. The benefits of idolatry were immediate, while the consequences were generally more long term. Idolatry was created when I spiritually compromised because my objectivity had eroded. I sought strict pleasure at the expense of loving discipline. Through rebelliousness, I perched guilt and shame upon my self-made thrones.

Idolatry thrived on my misguided affections and ignorance and was an end run around God's sovereignty. Idolatry is the source of many human illusions and pretensions. Idol worship, which is basically a worship of self, has an irrational base and reveals what we really live for. We have a tendency to worship creatures (of habit) rather than our Creator.

According to Yael Danieli, "The worshiper of an idol donates confessional status to it, which is exactly the idol's hidden power." My ignorance only gave it more power. When I fashioned and sustained an idol, I was guilty of inappropriate bonding and false identification. I had carved my own god through false beliefs, because I wasn't very vigilant in regard to the devotion of my time, focus, and energy. Idols are pretenders and impostors.

Danieli suggests that when a death occurs, our burdened and heavy hearts can become a graveyard to the deceased. Grasping and clinging to the guilt is a way of maintaining these internally carried graveyards. It is feared that successful mourning and grieving will lead to forgetting the dead and thereby committing them to oblivion. Therefore, guilt may serve a commemorative role and as an expression of loyalty to the dead. Much of my guilt was an unconscious form of an after-the-fact loyalty to Tina. I had to maintain a sense of honor in some capacity.

Survival guilt counteracted feelings of injustice and loneliness by helping provide a sense of belonging to the community that experienced the event. In my sense of survivor guilt, I was grateful for being alive, but at the same time I felt intense sorrow for Tina and her grieving family members. The wrong person had survived, and I didn't know why. Beating the so-called survival odds made no sense unless I had earned it in some way. I perceived my healing to be at the expense of Tina, and then I felt the obligation of guilt to her.

My feelings seemed so trivial, especially compared to her death. I experienced guilt for having any feelings at all, and then I became more reluctant to express them. Survivor guilt helped me cope with the feelings of helplessness and powerlessness. Within the suffering, I often thought of life before the tragic event that led to more feelings of guilt. Tragedy made me realize the value of how things used to be. Through guilt, I had a tendency to drive back time and permanently park.

Guilt also reminded me of the times in my nightmare(s) when I frantically yelled to get the others' attention right before impact. Why couldn't just one person hear me? Often, I was unfair to myself by trying to use the knowledge I had after the fact to a second in time when the information did not exist or was not in my awareness. These are two distinct planes that should not be compared. I didn't have the benefit of any time machines. Therefore, logic or persuasion had little impact on my sense of guilt as a whole. Being told by several well-meaning people that it was just an accident made me feel like nobody was listening to me. Quite frankly, when people came up with such easy answers, it made me feel ignorant and/or it convinced me of their ignorance in spite of their good intentions.

Another "benefit" of guilt was discovering that I had an unconscious desire to be admired for feeling guilty. My supporting role was heightened in an effort to counter balance the reality of guilt. By staying focused on the guilt, it became a way to avoid other unresolved issues and emotions, too. Dan Allender writes that a facade of guilt can become a self-centered effort to escape the wound, and the potential for more criticism, disapproval, or judgment. When seen or observed as guilt-ridden, people are less likely to confront us.

Although the nature of guilt wanted to isolate me, the answers were not found in segregation. I needed to deviate from both my human nature and the nature of false guilt by using only a supernatural power to overcome the emotional quagmire. Although guilt should not be worshipped, it should be respected.

I needed to open myself to a relationship with God and become aware of my maladaptive ways of coping. Failure to do so meant separation from the truth, which would prevent any significant healing. Awareness implies vigilance in observing or insight in drawing inferences from our experiences. But awareness is only half the battle; it is often useless if not attached to some change in behavior. It does not always motivate someone to change. As an example, the speed limit sign on the side of a highway has no significant meaning to many drivers. The person who is aware of his flaws is open to God's love and presence because he realizes he is not God. Our flaws do not need to threaten us. Harold Kushner writes: "Although God may be disappointed in some of the things we do, He is never disappointed in who we are, fallible people struggling with the implications of knowing good and evil."[1]

Perfectionism

"When perfectionism is paramount, the comparison of self with others, inevitably ends in the self feeling lesser for the comparison."

Gershen Kaufman

According to Kushner, God did not ask Abraham to be perfect or not to make a mistake, but to be whole. Similarly, we don't need to give up on people, but we do need to give up our unrelenting quest for perfection. God doesn't expect perfect obedience, but He is looking for us to have a living faith. Perfectionism is a sign of insecurity and a quest for possessive control. It also made me prone to more guilt and shame. Perfectionism's curse and strain was all about me trying to play God. It was rooted in a childhood of chaos and was an overcompensation of the adult child who was trying to prevent being hurt again. As a child, I assumed the hurt was because someone else in authority had control; but now as an adult and as an authority figure myself, I would have complete command.

Perfection is a divine attribute, but it is an impossible human attainment. According to Georgia Witkin, "It is not noble to want perfection; it is cruel. We could spend the rest of our lives feeling guilty or we can accept our imperfections as part of what is real."[2] The perfectionistic person is, in effect, a legalist. Dr. Bruce Narramore and Bill Counts tell us, "Although the Bible gives us guidelines, they are not enough for the insecure person. He cannot trust the internal guidance of the Holy Spirit, so he must seek detailed external rules to relieve his feelings of inadequacy. Legalistic rules fit right into our need for security."[3]

I was bound for more disappointment because of the unrealistic and impossible demands I had set for myself. Perfectionism is the opposite of trust and grace. In the words of Ernest Kurtz and Katherine Ketcham, "Imperfection is the wound that lets God in." It is a blessing to be imperfect. It was easier for me to follow a set of rules than to be left feeling defenseless. The rules were my suits of armor whose texture was firm and impenetrable.

I had taken the internal demand of perfection upon myself because I was convinced that acceptability and loveability were at stake, although perfectionism only guarantees that we will not fit in. And little did I know that my internal demands were based on erroneous external myths. They were unrealistic attempts to compensate for the perceived deficiencies in myself. Perfectionists also have a ready-made system of guilt or shame that comes into play whenever they feel they are not "measuring up" to the demands they have selected or learned.

Perfectionism actually denied my appropriate guilt, shame, and my own limits of being a human being. I needed to incorporate Alfred Adler's phrase into my life and have "the courage to be imperfect." Perfectionism made it harder for me to let go of the guilt. A sense of self-importance developed because it became more satisfying to endure and hang onto the guilt than to accept myself as flawed or ordinary.

Perfectionism bred a compulsive lifestyle focused on the externals and extremes of life. Because of all or nothing thinking, average was to be avoided at all costs. Perfectionistic thinking and reasoning bred many of my self-defeating beliefs. Virtually no pressure exists in being genuine, as opposed to being perfect. Being genuine is much more likely to put me in a warm crowd of legitimate friends. Perfectionism left me cold, fearful, lonely, and spiritually paralyzed. The sheer loneliness had deafening echoes that would never be answered until I cried out to God. My sense of loneliness was more directly related to the depth that I knew and acknowledged God. Loneliness was also one of God's ways of getting my attention.

I finally discovered that guilt had covered my biggest need. In the words of Lewis Smedes, "What I felt most was a glob of unworthiness that I could not tie down to any concrete sins I was guilty of. What I needed more than pardon was a sense that God accepted me, owned me, held me, affirmed me, and would never let go of me even if He was not too impressed with what He had on His hands."[4]

- 8 -

CONQUERING SHAME

*"Because the Sovereign Lord helps me, I will
not be disgraced. Therefore have I set my face like
flint, and I know I will not be put to shame."*
                                                Isaiah 50:7

As I continued to read at the hospital chapel, my
focus slowly evolved from guilt to shame. It was easy to
identify what I had done wrong, but it was much more
difficult to distinguish who I was and how I felt about
myself as a whole. Although I wasn't aware of it, shame
had a much stronger impact on me than guilt. Its roots
were from a much earlier time than the immediate
aftermath of the accident.

Shame is a normal emotion designed to tell us of our
human traits as compared to God's. It is a basis for
humility before God. Healthy shame lets us know when
we are separated from God. Carl Scheider says, "The
function of shame is to preserve wholeness and
integrity." The Bible specifically mentions shame over
130 times. Before their sin, Adam and Eve felt no shame

for their nakedness because of their trust in God. Once trust was broken through disobedience (seeking to be like God), the first emotions Adam and Eve felt were guilt and shame. Guilt put the two into a state where they knew they were wrong, while shame led to their behavior of hiding. They were ashamed of their nakedness and of the fact that they acted against God's will. Shame is the traumatic exposure of our various forms of nakedness. The root of the word "shame" means "to cover." Shame is considered more potent than guilt because it tends to be more focused on the sense of self rather than on a specific act. Generally, guilt is what we feel when we make a mistake. Shame can make us feel like we are a mistake.

Toxic Shame

Emotional problems arise when a person allows his shame to be changed or enmeshed into a state of being, and the shame itself becomes the basis for a person's identity. This is exactly what happened to me. Shame is an emotion and is not designed to be a state of being like righteous guilt. Once it becomes a state of being, shame loses its divine and functional purpose and becomes toxic. Repressed shame creates and maintains separation from people and the real self, not to mention God.

Toxic shame, a breach from the real self, is based on various forms of perceived rejection, betrayal, and broken trust. For me, it felt like a wound made from the inside. Shame is also a relationship wound. I became convinced it was a feeling of remorse about my own being and that virtually everyone had negative feelings toward me. This type of shame sears and shatters the soul. Because of toxic shame, I had an antagonistic relationship with myself.

My inner script of shame began to form well before the accident when, as a child, I began to identify with my shame-based father. Children always remember their parents' worst behavior. I had great difficulty creating an identity, because I lacked consistent and constructive feedback from my parents. For all three children, premature exposure to the elements within our dysfunctional home bred the toxicity of shame.

I also identified with my mother who unconsciously enabled my father's drinking. She was often intimidated by his shame, insecurities, and violent behavior, and she was unable to form and sustain any consistent boundaries. I related to her passivity, denial, and reluctance to make any significant change. It was easy to be angry at my father, but it was very difficult to acknowledge any anger or disappointment toward my mother without feeling disloyal or unappreciative of her loving efforts. She literally caught hell from my father more than any of the children combined, and it was easier to feel sorry for her.

The toxic shame remained a secret, which placed my soul in a conflicted state. I would need to involve others as I exposed my secret(s) to Christ. Shame, like guilt, is best released through the process of confession. I needed to break the tomb-like silence of shame by talking and praying about it. The irony of shame was that hiding and concealing my vulnerabilities only increased their power.

Toxic shame prefers justice over forgiveness, and it became an unconscious curse. Philosopher Jean Paul Sartre calls shame a "hemorrhage of the soul." Similarly, in regard to confessing sin, Dietrich Bonhoeffer writes, "The expressed acknowledged sin has lost all its power. It has been revealed and judged as sin. A person is no longer alone with his evil for he has cast off his sin in confession and handed it over to God."[1] With each series of confessions, shame's intensity was lessened.

Before my mother's death, we were able to resolve many lingering issues that we both had been afraid to acknowledge. She took the initiative in our conversation(s) and demonstrated, again, how much courage and class she had. This cherished time with her was a very significant and meaningful blessing in my life. She achieved peace in her life long before I ever did.

Looking back several years after the accident, I chose not to confess the toxic shame, and it empowered many addictive behaviors. Other false gods or love affairs included invincibility and the malignancy of approval and control. But these forms of behavior only heaped more shame upon me as they failed to deliver. Acting out the shame through the use of alcohol was my most desperate attempt in trying to escape from it. I was on the verge of following my father's wayward path. I was treacherously close to living the words of Paul in Romans 7:15, "I do not understand what I do. For what I want to do I do not do, but what I hate I do." Likewise, Alice Miller has shown that much "criminal behavior is 'acting out' behavior, and is a reenactment in which an offender criminalizes today in similar ways he was once victimized."

After years of more study and reflection, I learned that super-critical people have heavy amounts of internalized shame. Their focus is on finding fault outside themselves. Self-righteousness is a way to avoid awareness of their own flaws and failures because they unconsciously fear looking inside themselves. In short, people use feeling superior to others to avoid feeling badly about themselves. My perfectionistic traits would compel me to try to live flawlessly in order to avoid any criticism that could elicit more shame.

Narcissism

Narcissism derives its roots from "the beautiful youth of Greek legend who fell in love with his reflection in a pool and pined away in rapture over it."

Otto Kernberg

I hadn't realized how egotistical my need for self-punishment had become. Unknowingly, I became self-absorbed through the guilt and shame. It's embarrassing to admit, but I had more narcissistic traits than I was willing to admit to myself, much less to others. I think it is safe to say we all have some narcissistic traits. These traits are overcompensations for what truly lurks beneath. Many people refuse to be themselves because they don't like themselves. Their masks hide their insecurities. Someone who is always talking about himself and his achievements is probably a person who is, in his unconscious, feeling rejected and unwanted. In the words of E. Joseph Cossman, "A person all wrapped up in himself generally makes a pretty small package."

Narcissistic traits make up a complex network of survival strategies. These traits include an exaggerated sense of self-importance, a general lack of empathy (for anyone other than self), a sense of entitlement, working people through various forms of manipulation, and a constant need to fish for admiration. One is often preoccupied with fantasies of power, brilliance, and unlimited success to counter and feed his ego-dominated reality. A response to criticism may include marked feelings of shame, inferiority, humiliation, emptiness, or rage. The rage is often an (un)conscious attempt to make the issue about the other person, i.e., "How could you?" which tries to deflect the accountability off of the narcissist's behavior. Intensity within relationships is virtually always a must. At this point, I was pulled toward intensity like a magnet.

These traits are rooted in a childhood where love may have been conditional and/or where there was no genuine love. Specifically, it is found in the infant's early emotional adaptation. The present-day adult has never internalized an affectionate object, thus a sense of inner emptiness is created. They may feel unloved and unwanted from birth but can't understand why. Rather than asking such an embarrassing question, many people learn to keep quiet to control the potential embarrassment or humiliation. This is one reason many people are terrified of their intense childhood feelings.

Narcissistic behavior prefers to possess, rather than love, because equality and intimacy are a threat to their sense of control. Love is too risky. Arrogance is directly linked to unconscious narcissistic traits. In their minds, humility is a form of weakness; but spiritual brokenness is exactly what is needed to experience life-changing grace and forgiveness. Humility is reached when we accept ourselves as small (not insignificant). Only when I became honest with myself about my selfishness, did I begin to start taking power from it. Narcissism crumbles before grace. Proverbs 16:18 says, "Pride goes before destruction, a haughty spirit before a fall."

Under the pretense of grandiosity, narcissism confines the genuine self within the walls of the false self. Narcissistic behavior includes a sense of over sensitivity, inner restlessness, and a readiness to feel toxic shame and guilt. Dependence is bred by learning to perform flawlessly in every endeavor or simply by not attempting to try. Impressive facades are admired, not the genuine person they could be. They are often envious of whole people because they don't have to make constant efforts to earn admiration. They never allow themselves to be ordinary. It is simply unacceptable. Many of their prior external achievements have actually hindered their inner healing.

Narcissistic wounds heal through the mourning of unfulfilled childhood dreams and expectations. Healing begins when we become aware of what we have lost. Jesus allowed and used the sordid ugliness of the accident to help show me what I had missed and to expose my weaknesses, which had been previously unknown.

Co-Dependency

Many believe the foundation of the buzzword "co-dependency" begins once shame is internalized. A key difference between guilt and shame emerges. A guilty person generally wants to make amends. On the other hand, the shame-based person wants to be punished. In my sense of guilt, I wanted punishment. With shame, I feared abandonment. There is usually relief in confessing most guilt, but my fear of further abandonment prevented the confession of the shame. At this critical juncture, I falsely attained acceptability by others' reactions to me. My worth and value had become dependent upon what others might say or do. I needed external affirmations because of the internal shame.

I learned much later that we have divine worth because we are made in God's image, not because of anything outside of us (Genesis 1:26-27). The shame-based person has virtually no inner life or intimacy because they lack consistent emotional boundaries. Their lifestyle consists of caring for the emotional and physical needs of others. They thrive on too much responsibility, at the expense of their own feelings, dignity, and overall well-being. Co-dependent behavior is often caused by being raised in an emotionally and spiritually hostile environment where safety is a chronic fear. I concur with Robert Burney when he said, "We grew up denying the reality of what was happening in our home and denying our feelings of what we were experiencing." Co-dependency's power may not be fully reflected until we are in adult relationships.

In a shame-based family, "average" rarely exists. Present-day adults have a tendency toward the extremes of overachieving or underachieving. Solomon described such over achievements as "meaningless, a chasing after the wind" (Ecclesiastes 2:11). Achievements, alone, do not fill the void in our lives and may only increase our frustration. Simply put, there was a sense of emptiness I could never fill.

Like guilt, I needed shame to help guide my behavior. Shame can be viewed as another emotional regulator, a check-and-balance mechanism. It appears that lack of shame is one of the biggest burdens and problems in society today. Our culture of shamelessness is steeped in our overall sense of irreverence. Someone once said if you never feel shame, you've either become totally divine or evil. In the words of Blaine Pascal, "The only shame is to have none."

Initially following the accident, I focused strictly on how to distance myself from the shame rather than trying to understand its divine and functional purpose. I was learning that shame is actually an invitation to grace. Later, grace would represent the ultimate show-down with my sense of shame. Appropriate shame leads to redemptive desire and helps prevent the perils of self-absorption.

The Generational Curse of Shame

Today, when I think of shame, the first person who comes to mind is my father. One of his favorite ways to verbally punish me was to use the unforgettable phrase, "I'd be ashamed." This deeply entrenched adage was one of many reasons I took criticism of my actions as judgments of myself. Other people's judgment exercised a paralyzing effect. The fear of any criticism prevented me from showing and expressing myself freely.

My father suffered through many humiliating, shameful acts and beatings at the hands of his father. I've been told my grandfather suffered multiple beatings in his childhood, too. The power of generational curses should never be underestimated. My father ran away from home at the age of 17 to escape the abuse. I wish I could say he never looked back, but in many ways, it was all he ever did. He was haunted by the events that happened in his own home and backyard. Through his repressed emotions, he brought an endless amount of shame and rage into our family, which he violently expressed through the use of alcohol. Shame completely dominated my father. My dad dealt with the shame through several dysfunctional behaviors: smoking up to three packs of cigarettes a day, eating excessively, drinking too much, and often losing his volatile temper. For the majority of his life, acting out the shame only reinforced his feelings of insecurity. As Donald Nathanson puts it, "Shame is the shaper of symptoms."

Many of my co-dependent traits attempted to compensate for the shame of having a chemically-dependent father. My need to "protect" him from the consequences of his use was attributed to my need to hide the disgraceful and shameful reality from the outside world. In short, our family felt the consequences of my father's drinking behavior more than he did. In reality, the caregivers got in the way and buffered him from those consequences. Thus, my father actually became less motivated to change because he didn't have to. He may have lost respect for us (unconsciously) because we tolerated too much. Caregivers may need to make some changes in their own behavior first before they can realistically expect any significant change from the other person. In a universal example, the co-dependent doesn't become sick because of the alcoholic, but rather is attracted to the alcoholic because of his own sickness. Because co-dependents are addicted to guilt and shame, living a lie becomes their way of life.

Co-dependency traits are by-products of our experiences. We all have some co-dependent traits. Some of the most generous, sensitive, bright, and wonderful people are those with co-dependent traits. But the biggest problem with these traits, rather than having them, is not being aware of them. A side effect of shame was that it hampered my self-awareness. It made me feel like I was in the middle of a dense fog, which prevented me from seeing anyone, while at the same time, it prevented anyone from seeing me. Thus, my problem was more about my perception and not necessarily my vision.

Compulsive rescuers tolerate abuse and shoveled shame. Due to their lack of objectivity, they become confused because they aren't "rewarded" for their toler-ance. They are more likely to be reactors rather than initiators. Reacting is safer for the co-dependent. Others dictate their behavior and feelings, whether good or bad. The act of following can be a passive-aggressive way of trying to control the leader because if a mistake is made, the follower can attempt to insulate and buffer himself from responsibility. Initiative requires assertiveness without fear of rejection, but rejection is one of the most dominant forms of power for people who have not yet become mature Christians. The risk of initiative may be avoided at all costs. On the other hand, the key to becoming a quality Christian is learning to follow. We were created to follow Christ.

People with a compulsion to please and control tend to live life in its extreme and exaggerated forms. They settle for all or nothing, black or white, with no grey allowed. They do not see that they are victims of another's cruelty and guilt. Because they are addicted to human approval and affirmation, it's hard for them to tell the truth or to hear it from another because they fear disapproval.

My biggest co-dependent trait was centered on approval. First, it was manifested in the endless efforts to win my father's elusive approval. His constant yelling was literally taken to heart. It was an unsettling reminder of his disappointment and anger with his own father. Second, approval was sought through my generally passive attitude, and reluctance to make and sustain any major changes that I may have learned from my mother. Third, these traits were best illustrated in trying to win the approval of self and others following the accident. Could I ever be accepted by people again, after what I had done? Could I ever be at peace with myself?

I made a big mistake in becoming too enamored with meaningless earthly attachments, such as people's opinions, instead of God's Word. I needed to stop being a pleaser and depending on others to give me an identity. Richard Foster states, "Because we lack a Divine center our need for security has led us into an insane attachment to things. We crave things we neither need nor enjoy...It is time we awaken to the fact that conformity to a sick society is to be sick."[2]

It is tough to escape the recrimination laid upon us by the perceived or assumed judgment of society as a whole. There are always people who, out of their own chaos and insecurities, want to manipulate our lives and feelings. They criticize conduct and breed shame, intent on producing guilt and conformity. We need to find security in Romans 12:2 which says, "Do not conform any longer to the pattern of this world, but be transformed by the renewing of your mind."

It was awkward to identify my feelings because I had learned that many of my feelings were wrong or shameful. In childhood, if I were allowed to express my feelings, it was often viewed as talking back, and I ran the risk of losing my father's love or approval. Seen through a child's eyes of perfectionism, over-responsibility, and repressed emotions, my perspective toward God was easily distorted. I often felt God had me under constant surveillance to find what I was doing wrong, rather than the idea that He was observing to protect and love me. My efforts were endless, but the increased intensity and commitment often resulted in more introspection, compulsion, and detachment rather than more intimacy, calmness, and reassurance.

Without intending to, I placed myself in performance traps following the accident. I tried to atone for what I had done. To think I could possibly "make up" for my mistake(s) was an insult to God's grace. These attempts to correct the mistakes were other examples of my innate selfishness. In short, I was seeking approval through the wrong dimension.

Because I was a survivor of a low-nurturance childhood, I was more prone to guilt and shame. And because of the conflicting and inconsistent messages, I had internalized the wrong message about acceptance and rejection. Words have the power to hurt or heal; verbal abuse or neglect can be more debilitating than physical abuse. Bruises heal faster than the wounds inflicted by verbal abuse. Often I remembered and lived the words I heard more than the actions I observed. As I grew older, I insatiably craved strokes to compensate for the very few affirmations I heard as a child. But the constant yearning for repeated human validation contradicted or devalued the contentment I should have had with God's approval. Looking back, I can see myself in the words of John 12:43, "For they loved praise from men more than praise from God."

God wanted me to take the lead, but I would not turn loose the reins to accept what He wanted to do for me. My need for validation really worked against me. I made the mistake of carrying this earthly life baggage and trying to transpose it into my new spiritual walk. But God doesn't work that way. I was learning that I needed to adjust to God more than God needed to adjust to me.

Brennan Manning points out that a poor self-image actually reveals a lack of humility. Feelings of inferiority and inadequacy help keep our attention focused on ourselves. Manning states, "Humble people, rather than a low opinion of themselves, have no opinion of themselves, because they so rarely think about themselves. Humility is manifested in an indifference to our well-being and the image we present. A humble man does not fear being exposed."[3]

The work of acquiring my worth had already been done at Christ's Crucifixion. The Crucifixion needed to have more meaning in my life. If I were to achieve universal approval (which I can't), I would be as sick as the entire gamut of sin manifested in human nature. We have a universal need for forgiveness and restoration, not for people's approval. My freedom was lost through pleasing behaviors. In this context, my good friend and pastor, Bill Kierce, may have said it best when he stated, "We are most like God when we seek to serve, but we are least like Him when we seek to please." I wasn't created solely for the earth's approval but for God's approval through my own sense of being.

Guilt and comparison are the top two methods used to master and manipulate shame-based people. Many people primarily reason from their emotion, allowing their feelings (heart) to take precedence over their brain's logic. People with co-dependent traits often confuse love with pity and tend to "love" people they can pity and rescue. Rescuing gives them a heightened sense of meaning, because the rescue is more for their benefit: to feel needed and to develop their sense of belongingness. Pity can be very intoxicating and seducing, too. Shame-filled people can become enmeshed with their parent's, partner's, or even their child's needs and emotions.

At the time of the accident, still ensnarled with my father's issues, I had not developed any sense of a whole identity. Still strictly my father's son, I had not come of age to become my own person. Plus, the Heavenly Father's dynamics hadn't even come into conscious play. Emotionally, I was still treating and assuming both fathers were one and the same: distant, detached and preoccupied with other more important matters.

I was to discover that "religion" can also become a defense against the feeling of shame. But this defense not only masks but falsifies reality. Initially, I inadvertently used Scripture as a means to avoid reality rather than trying to face it. Functionally, this defense also serves to deflect one's own sense of shame and project it onto others. In this context, often in the first few moments after we've met someone, the more times they mention God may be indicative of how unhealthy they are.

In my reading years later, I found some much need clarification. As Mike Mason writes: "There is a thin line between admiration or worship of the Deity and jealousy of Him, between the hunger to be like God and the hunger to be God. Religion seeks in holiness an antidote to sin and evil; irreligion seeks in superhumanness an antidote to God."[4] Our sinful human nature gives us the desire to play or rival God. We feel less vulnerable if we are in control. If we are in power, it is also much easier to transfer our sense of shame to another person, attempting to eliminate any shame-inducing experiences for ourselves.

Another paradox for shame-filled people is that they are actually being controlled by the persons they are trying to control. For years, I had tried to control my father in an attempt to stop the insanity occuring in our house. Control in this context is not necessarily about power but about a mean(s) to attain safety and predictability. Underneath the controlling and manipulative behavior we usually see a very frightened person.

Withdrawal and isolation are also used as defenses against shame. "If you can't find me, you can't shame me" can become a person's slogan. But now, one is more susceptible to self-destructive tendencies. Isolation is a perilous condition, and we go behind enemy lines when we retreat into isolation.

- 9 -

Receiving the Blessing

"Oh, that you would bless me and enlarge my
territory! Let your hand be with me, and keep me
from harm so that I will be free from pain."
I Chronicles 4:10

I didn't learn much about the term "blessing" until
years later when I began my clinical supervision under
Dr. Myron Madden. This experience, too, was another
valuable step in my journey to wholeness. I discovered
that a blessing from a parent is the consistent message of
unconditional love for the child(ren). It's the whole
message of acceptance, validation, encouragement,
nurturance, guidance, warmth, and safety. To bless is to
invoke divine care for. Ideally, it is something we should
know and feel when we first think of authority. But I
had an altogether different view of authority because of
the influence of alcohol. God limits much of His
blessing(s) to come through some human channel.
Generally, it is through a parent, but it can come from
anyone the child authorizes.

Our first concept of God is usually through our first father figure. And that is big! A.W. Tozer says, "What comes into our mind when we first think of God is the most important thing about us." We are created to receive God's blessing, and His blessing is based upon our being (image) rather than our doing (performance). If we continue to measure and compare ourselves, Terry Kellogg states, we are in danger of becoming a "human doing" rather than a human being. Jesus' desire to bestow His blessings upon us is reflected in his words to the criminal by his side, "I tell you the truth, today you will be with me in paradise" (Luke 23:43).

Myron Madden shares, "The chief blessing of the family is that of preparing us to go beyond family." Psychologically speaking, theorizes Madden, "We need to sever the chord and strings that bind us in emotional dependence on parents, siblings, and the extended family. The only way the wonderful world beyond family can be opened to us comes in closing that door behind you."[1] And nobody can close that door for you. We separate from our parent(s) to make our own decisions and choose our own values.

In my case, the lack of healthy separation would plague me for years. It was very difficult to leave a dysfunctional home because of all the excess baggage. In essence, I had to make several trips back in order to process the remaining baggage claims. Unfortunately, many insecure parents refuse to allow their children to leave. The way to ensure this is to withhold the blessing through conditional love. Conditional love breeds shame.

> "Love is the birthright of every person."
> Mother Teresa

Detach and Disengage

> "Blessed are all who take refuge in him."
> Psalm 2:12

We may need to detach and disengage from our imperfect parent(s). This doesn't mean we shouldn't have a relationship or that we should ignore them. Ignoring only antagonizes people. If done correctly, the parent(s) may not even be aware of our healthy detachment. We simply stop looking to our parents for things they can't give us. Until I realized my father didn't have a full blessing to give, I stayed emotionally attached, performing to get the blessing that would never come. At that time, he couldn't give me what he never received.

Many adults are still striving to attain the elusive approval by measuring up. Their parents' yardstick, however, is warped, cracked, and splintered. These adults suffer needlessly throughout their lives from oppressive feelings of guilt and shame for not having lived up to their parents' impossible expectations or demands. The compulsion toward the illusory approval can intensify following a parent's death by a child's magnified and unabashed loyalty to the dead. Often, we are prone to deify our loved ones following their death. Following my father's death, I had a tendency to grieve more for what he could have been and what we could have had.

We do need to forgive our parents for being weak, flawed, and selfish just like the rest of us. For the same reason, we hope our children will forgive us for the mistakes we have made and will make in the future. Earlier, I had lost respect for my father. But over the years, I would develop a newer, fresher respect for him through the dynamics of grace and forgiveness. My parents didn't give me everything I needed as a child, but they gave me all they had. Now, like any other child, it's up to me to make the most of what I did receive. They simply weren't capable of giving me all I needed. But no parent is. Forgiving our parents may be the only way we can honor them (Exodus 20:12). Shame can swindle us out of some of our childhood and adulthood because of broken trust, but grace gives it back or lets us discover it for the first time.

The process of receiving the blessing may take a great deal of time. It has taken years for me. My father's alcoholism and the trauma of the accident derailed most of my maturation process. My parents' loving words before their impending deaths were monumental for me in being fully blessed by them. One of the biggest keys in receiving the fullness of God's blessing was the realization that my parents were just like everybody else, no more and no less. As I became more comfortable with this truth, I became hungrier for God's truth.

The bounty of the blessing will always defeat the shadows of shame. In my previous experience(s) with blessing, I felt I needed Tina's blessing, too. At one point, I valued her blessing more than anyone's, including God's. I came to understand they are actually one and the same. A blessing from heaven has only one source. I'm not sure why, but I never hesitated in my belief that Tina would forgive me. This discernment was much more than just a strong sense of wishful thinking. I later discovered Tina had an active faith; she was a member of a local Catholic church. If a person's spirit is in heaven, how could they not forgive? Ultimately, I wanted her forgiveness for my actions, but I needed my parents' blessing for my being. Now, for the first time in my life, I felt I was in the process of receiving both.

As important as blessings are, we also need to value brokenness. It is our first step in transcending shame. Brokenness is not to be confused with complete destruction. Brokenness is the awareness and ability to acknowledge our helplessness. It is a requirement of grace. Destruction is a direct result of refusing to allow or admit to ourselves the need to be broken. Grace would allow me to move beyond disgrace and the need to respond with or in shame. One blessing I did have (a universal blessing for us all) was that all of my previous bad choices in life could be redeemed by a single good choice. One theological aspect could be, "If it's not broke, break it!" Broken people are one step closer to Christ and healing.

Rejecting Toxic Shame Through Acceptance

While shame is not necessarily an ailment to be cured, like guilt, it is a vital catalyst in my humanness. When understood and experienced appropriately, both are forms of self-evaluation. In other words, I needed to experience it, share it, and to positively change because of it. This is the whole meaning of guilt and shame. They are divinely designed to be instructive by nature. Shame is ultimately related to virtue.

Because I was accepted by God, I no longer feared rejection or abandonment to the extent that they immobilized me. In short, I eliminated the threat of toxic shame through God's acceptance. Toxic shame directly contradicts God's image because the shame is based on human perceptions and not God's. The root of my toxic shame was pride because I rejected myself as God created me to be. Pride and shame can be considered paradoxical sisters. In the words of Max Lucado, "If pride is what goes before a fall, then shame is what keeps you from getting up after one."

God honored my worth as He overlooked my undeserving. The Lord and the Holy Spirit converted my guilt and shame by changing my inner self. But this process would progress at a snail's pace. My identity was found through God's pardon, acceptance, and grace. Understanding, believing, and living God's acceptance would be a cherished threshold in my journey toward wholeness. God continues to celebrate and console me each and every step of the way.

Jesus endured the shame of all the leaders and then shamed them by revealing their true hearts. He overcame guilt and shame through the power of suffering and creative love. Shame itself was crucified. While He hung mercilessly upon the cross and through knowing joy awaited Him in heaven, Jesus was able to bear His shame on earth. Hebrews 12:2 says, "Fix our eyes on Jesus, the author and perfecter of our faith, who for the joy set before him endured the cross, scorning its shame, and sat down at the right hand of the throne of God."

In the words of Frank Lake, "He hangs on the Cross naked. Both the innocent and the guilty are ashamed. Both have something to hide. He is identified with the innocent in nakedness. Deprived of His natural clothing, men shrank away from Him. The whole world will see this same King appearing in all His beauty and glory, because He allowed both...to be utterly taken away."[2]

Finally, I was breaking away and letting myself off my self-made hook. Slowly, the absence of false guilt and toxic shame began to produce a keen sense of boldness combined with the power of acceptance, creating a sense of inner joy. In other words, I was beginning to allow God to love all of me for the first time.

What God declares, the believing heart confesses without the need of further proof. Everyone who possesses the gift of faith will recognize the wisdom in the daring words of one of the early church fathers: "I believe that Christ died for me because it is incredible; I believe that He rose from the dead because it is impossible."[3]

- 10 -

RECEIVING GRACE

"For it is by grace you have been saved, through faith—and this not from yourselves, it is the gift of God."

Ephesians 2:8

In dealing with guilt and shame, I was led to a theological concept about which I had very little knowledge. Grace had been a foreign object in my world. In my mind, grace was one of those sophisticated church words that didn't really apply to the real world, not to mention my current circumstances. I was a miserable Christian who did not fully understand all the aspects of His grace. But I was on the brink of a life-changing higher education experience that would dramatically alter the landscape of my paltry understanding of grace as a whole.

In my reading and later studies, I learned that grace is a free and abundant gift unearned by guilty sinners, and it is far grander and more costly than I could ever imagine. It is God's most generous gift to us. Grace, received through faith, is an active and effective power of God's love, which brings merciful aid to people. Grace is God's eternal covenant with us. It is our anglicized form of the Greek word *charis*, which means "graciousness, kindness, a favor." Grace is also what God does when He meets my imperfections, sins, and failures. Grace is God's gift to overcome my guilt and toxic shame. Through grace, I unknowingly inherited an infinite number of God's promises.

Grace came to include the idea of "condescending favor." The word is based on the old Hebrew term which means "to bend, to stoop." The late pastor and Bible scholar, Donald Barnhouse, perhaps said it best: "Love that goes upward is worship; love that goes outward is affection; love that stoops is grace."[1] Grace describes God's mysterious healing, restoring, redeeming, and reconciling nature. Although I did not always feel it, I was always in the presence of God's grace, regardless of the circumstance. We find dignity, freedom and peace through grace. The word gracious is marked by a generosity of spirit, and describes a person who is approached with ease and who responds pleasantly.

Discovering grace in our "remembering when" is related to what we are looking for in our memories, which can haunt or bless us. As we tell each other our memories, we can discover our inner strength growing. Up to this point, I hadn't shared anything with other people. My emotionally-guarded condition immediately following the accident had lingered and was now doing more harm than good.

God's grace is at work in this sharing. To withdraw from people is to withdraw from the primary source God uses to give us grace. David Augsburger clarifies by saying, "People's stories give us a sense of vision. We turn our pain into narrative so we can bear it; we turn our ecstasy into narrative so we can prolong it."[2] Each of our stories needs another. Our stories unite with each other in solidarity. Every person has a valued story, scar, and joy to share. In the words of Isak Dinesan, "All sorrows can be borne if you put them in a story."

The grace of God is at work in all things. Although God empathized with me through all the bad which had occurred, He was more concerned about the good that was yet possible. God's perceived silence was in no way indicative of His activity, concern, love, or involvement during my distress. His best work is often behind the scenes in the various stages of my life. Grace is a constant—a firm, steadfast faithfulness.

Mercy and Pity

"But because of his great love for us, God, who is rich in mercy, made us alive with Christ even when we were dead in transgressions—it is by grace you have been saved."

Ephesians 2:4-5

I often used grace and mercy interchangeably. Although very similar, there is a distinct difference. God's goodness, freely given to the unworthy, is called grace; toward the suffering, it is called mercy or pity. God's grace gives me what I don't deserve. His mercy doesn't give me what I do deserve. Mercy is a blessing and is an act of divine compassion which forgoes punishment especially when justice demands it.

Grace implies a benign or gentle attitude and is a willingness to grant favors or make concessions. Christ, had He never become flesh, would have felt pity, but He could not have sympathized with His people to the fullest degree. In order to do just that, He decided to become man. Thus, He can relate to any person, in any

situation, because He's been there before. Hebrews 4:15
tells us, "For we do not have a high priest who is unable
to sympathize with our weaknesses, but we have one
who has been tempted in every way, just as we are—yet
was without sin."

Christ experienced physical and emotional abuse,
injustice, disloyalty, rejection, betrayal, neglect, abandonment, and was the object of others' rage, guilt, shame,
and ignorance. Randy Alcorn tells us, "Christ took the
hell He didn't deserve so we could have the heaven we
don't deserve."[3] Isn't it amazing Jesus would rather
experience hell for us than to go to heaven without us?
Isn't it remarkable God would rather sacrifice His Son
than to give up on you and me?

Pity is a sympathetic sorrow for one who is suffering.
Jesus made pity personal by suffering unjustly Himself.
Because He suffered, He has the full capacity for mercy
and pity. Self-pity serves a functional purpose as long as
we don't get swamped in it. We need to mourn for
ourselves just as God mourned for Christ. It's OK. My
problem with pity was the tendency to ultimately focus
on myself, whereas God was thinking of others all
along. Pity can be a dangerous partner.

Grace vs. Works

It was hard for me to rely on God's grace alone for
my salvation and emotional well-being. R.C. Sproul
states, "It is difficult for pride to rest on grace. Grace is
for other people—for beggars. We don't want to live by
a heavenly welfare system. We want to earn our own
way. We like to think that we will go to heaven because
we deserve to be there."[4] God's grace is for salvation,
but I needed it on a daily basis to discover more joy.
Salvation is not just a blessing we may receive on our
deathbed, but through His grace, it is to be rejoiced and

lived now. Grace would help prevent me from regressing to the old mental and physical behaviors, something my personality will always be prone to do. Spurgeon put it best when he said, "It is better to be leveled by grace than to be exalted by pride."

We all need the same amount of grace because the value of our good works is considered worthless before God. In a sense, good works have no more staying power than our bad works! After all God has done, our (over)works tell the Lord we still don't get it. Strict works can become a form of endless guilt-offerings and unintentional insults to His grace.

Grace isn't grace if it is given or withdrawn in response to human behavior. It's solely based on the sovereign goodness and purpose of God. Grace has nothing to do with me! My merit or demerit(s) has been made forever null and void. My works do not sway God to save me. If that were the case, my salvation would be based on a debit/credit system, and would leave grace powerless. Grace and (de)merit no more belong together than oil and water. Understanding grace would be the second most difficult learning adjustment to make in my new walk with God. I needed to have my earning mentality destroyed. I had been earning and striving all of my life. It's one thing to shift gears, but it is quite another to completely change vehicles and head in the opposite direction.

I cannot receive and give love unless I am experiencing grace. Grace is NOT cheap. Grace is unconditionally free to me, although infinitely expensive to God. This is grace in the fullness of its meaning. Grace does not ask questions nor does it set any limits. Since the cost of grace was infinite, the avenues of utilizing it are infinite.

Grace vs. (Out)laws

"I do not set aside the grace of God, for if righteousness could be gained through the law, Christ died for nothing!"

Galatians 2:21

According to the Bible, law and grace are opposite ways to approach God. Jesus changes the law(s) by changing people. The most basic difference between law and grace is how I would get God's acceptance. The law says: Perform so you will be accepted. Grace says: You are accepted, now you can perform. I often thought my sins were greater, uglier, and darker than God's ability to forgive them. Unknowingly, this was another form of pride. I needed to be humble enough to receive His grace and forgiveness. And adversity was what was humbling me the most. Andrew Murray states, "Pride must die in you, or nothing of heaven can live in you." I was unworthy of God's love based strictly upon my performance, but I was not worthless. In fact, you and I are priceless because of Christ's ultimate sacrifice for us.

Under law, I earn blessings. Under grace, God blesses me unconditionally, and I will want to obey Him. The law operates in large measure out of a fear motive. No matter how hard we try, we cannot legislate righteousness. In stark contrast, grace removes fearful anxiety, and replaces it with a love motive (I John 4:17-18). The law can expose sin, but only Jesus can remove it. Although the law shows what I have done wrong, it doesn't necessarily motivate me to do the right thing. Grace, on the other hand, always does. Grace changes the heart and the law becomes irrelevant. We do the right thing because of our heart and not because of the law.

Now, when I began to receive His grace, I began to trust. As a maturing Christian, I needed to ask the question, "What will love—not the law—allow me to do?" Incidentally, grace has always been offered even before the law existed. Because God knew us all too well, He made the necessary provisions before the fact, before the need. I was in the process of discovering that grace is retroactive. From God's perspective, we often ask for the impossible, but by His grace, we receive it. Charles Spurgeon writes of the value of grace by saying: "Grace is the soul and the music of the gospel; without it, the gospel is silent."

"Clearly no one is justified before God by the law, because, 'The righteous will live by faith.' Christ redeemed us from the curse of the law by becoming a curse for us..."
Galatians 3:11,13

Maybe God allowed me to go through the painful experiences of being rejected by people to appreciate what a miracle it is to be accepted by Him. Similarly, Willard Gaylin has written, "All of us must act selfishly to learn charity, must lie to learn honor, must betray and be betrayed to learn to value trust and commitment." These are telling examples of the evolvement of all events brought to God's ultimate conclusion through His grace.

Within the dynamics of acceptance is where I really struggled. For virtually all of my past and through the accident, primarily because of the influence of alcohol, I had never consistently experienced unconditional acceptance. It was a complete stranger to me. I had been starved for grace and didn't even know it. One reason the act of receiving God's grace was a struggle was because of old scars which were manifested in chronic patterns of being self-critical and feeling inadequate.

Even receiving a compliment, without automatically discounting it or allowing it to make me feel awkward, could be very tough. It was difficult just to say, "Thank you for being so kind."

God uses grace to relate to us. Grace became an interpersonal link between my experiences and God's acceptance. Being connected (not dependent) to other people provided the way to a liberating awareness that by grace, I was also accepted by God. It was incredible to believe I was accepted, with no strings attached or any fine print to concern myself with later. This was the moment when grace conquered all of my sins and I no longer felt estranged from God. And I had not done anything but trust God. Through trusting Him, I finally had the courage to accept acceptance. I needed to believe it. I had been granted instant clemency.

Embracing My Weaknesses

"My grace is sufficient for you, for my power is made perfect in weakness."

II Corinthians 12:9

As John Calvin said, "For men have no taste for it (God's power) until they are convinced of their need of it and they immediately forget its value unless they are continually reminded by awareness of their own weakness."[5] Human weakness and divine grace go hand in hand. It is within our weaknesses that God shows His powerful majesty. His Kingdom is clearly built on human weakness.

In God's sight, we are all totally and permanently, spiritually bankrupt. But His grace covers our bad checks. We are all guilty of a murder at Calvary. Martin Luther once said, "We actually carry His nails in our pockets." Jerry Bridges states, "To lose sight of our unworthiness or inadequacy is to risk exercising our gifts and fulfilling our ministries in a spirit of presumptuous pride, as if God were fortunate to have us on His team."[6] On the other hand, if I focus too much on my unworthiness, to the neglect of God's grace, I will immobilize myself for His service.

Grace Awareness

Indeed, we are weak, unworthy and inadequate. We are not bashing ourselves when we recognize this truth. In fact, the greater awareness we have of our weaknesses, the more aware we are of the power of His all sufficient grace. Similarly, the whole person is aware of his shortcomings, but is not threatened by them. A.W. Tozer states, "A meek person is not a human mouse afflicted with a sense of his own inferiority. He has accepted God's estimate of his own life. In himself, nothing; in God, everything. He knows the world will never see him as God sees him and he has stopped caring."[7]

What God expects of me is not in relation to the strength I have. Rather, it is in relation to the resources available that I find in Christ. I simply don't have the ability to accomplish the least of God's tasks. This is the cornerstone of grace. On the other hand, due to grace, there is nothing that God and I can't handle together. As Mother Teresa said, "I know God will not give me anything I can't handle. I just wish that He didn't trust me so much."

Because of my new grace awareness, I wanted to extend the same to others. The magnitude of grace began to set me free from all the entrapments of performance, and I found a new dimension of God's love that changed me forever. If I try to add any ingredient to His grace, I actually dishonor it. I accepted grace when I no

longer put strict confidence in myself. Spurgeon wisely
states, "Confidence in the self and reliance on the self
are bred in the bone—and will come out in the flesh."

Yes, we need self-confidence, but only under the
umbrella of what God says about us. We need Christ-
esteem and not self-esteem. Christ is the only person
who ever had an accurate view of Himself because of
His total dependence on God.

Truth and grace are actually interdependent, for
Jesus is the only whole example of them. God reveals
truth only to those people who genuinely seek it. Being
honest and candid with myself and others allowed me
to activate God's power. And although I could feel a
sense of pride for some of the positive changes I was
making in my life, I needed to understand that behavioral
change not rooted in grace is simply self-righteousness.
By accepting God's grace, I needed to give up my
omnipotent, God-like strivings and be reminded, "For
the battle is not yours, but God's" (2 Chronicles 20:15).

The human tendency is take the simple and make it
more complex. Common grace is, indeed, very simple—
too simple for many people to understand. My intellect
got in the way; it had been damaged spiritually and was
unable to fathom spiritual truth. The temptation was to
strictly trust my common sense. My common sense (just
as my conscience), though, came from a contaminated
and compromised pool of logic. Therefore, it was no
match for spiritual truth.

God's grace is not some kind of commodity He
rations out. Grace means a gracious God coming to me
with His loving arms open wide. God is on the move,
and I was learning He's one I can talk to, who talks and
listens to me; He's a God of compassion who did respond
to my needs. This is a promise (a fact) I could now base

my faith upon. Grace didn't just superficially skirt over my issues or make me feel good. It helped separate my real flaws versus those I had magnified or minimized. Grace also gave me the confidence to stretch myself in order to grow and mature.

Liberating Limits

Limits promote spiritual and emotional maturity. They clearly define my boundaries and are necessary in the formation of my identity. A limit is a prescribed maximum or minimum amount. When a train is limited, it offers superior and faster service. A limited edition of a book makes it a collectible. Limits set a point and also confine my mistakes. Adults certainly need limits, too. How we manage within our financial limitations is one of the most telling signs of spiritual maturity, especially when living within our means is counter to our culture.

God's self-imposed limits affect all of His children. He will be true to the limits for the overall benefit of each child. As Judith Viorst observes, "No is not a rejection, but it is a valued limitation. Limits may be a requirement for the creative development of our personality."[8] By becoming aware of my limitations, I began to learn of God's great power and sovereignty. It's like a batter trying to hit home runs when his strength is in being a singles hitter. He must play within himself and his capabilities. Many slumps begin when a batter tries to do too much and begins to press.

In one of Rev. Louise Westfall's sermons, she says that without Christ we face the harsh reality of the world like a hitter in a prolonged slump. Death is the power pitcher against which we cannot hit, not with love or money or health or all the skill in the world. But it is only through Christ that we can break death's

shutout record of consecutive scoreless innings. Through
Christ, life itself becomes a sacrifice fly. In essence, I was
learning the need to give myself up not only in order to
save myself, but also to eventually help bring a teammate
home.

- 11 -

THE VITAL CHURCH

"Now you are the body of Christ, and each one
of you is a part of it."

I Corinthians 12:27

In the vast majority of my past, the church was
where people got married and where funerals were
held. The church was just a hollow building with no
pulse. The few times I did go, my mind was often
preoccupied with the terror of the previous night. In my
mind, church people were out of touch with the real
world and couldn't really relate to what our family was
going through. If anybody was to discover our truth,
they would surely kick us out. We simply didn't belong,
but I wasn't going to tell anyone. I did not get help from
the church because I did not understand what it had to
offer.

Later, I learned the best place to witness grace is at
church, God's formal residence. Charles Morrison, perhaps the premier religious journalist of the early 20th
century, once said, "The church is the only institution in

the world whose membership is based on unworthiness." Feeling unworthy? Welcome to the church; join
us in our weakness. I need to have awareness and
maturity so that the sinful human element within the
church does not dictate the dynamics of my faith. The
extremes of others' behavior should not preclude me
from being fed and nourished. If so, I am empowering
their behavior over my own. In my case, it was the
extremes of my own behavior and rationale that prevented me from being fed. I learned a sobering lesson
that if I ever went hungry, it wasn't because God had
run out of food.

My distance from God was not as important as my
direction toward or away from Him. People who have
been hurt by the human element within the church are
some of the most difficult to reach. Accordingly, many
people don't go to church because "they've been there
before." Billy Sunday once wrote, "Many people can't
find God for the same reason that criminals can't find
the police. They aren't looking for them."

In spite of or because of human frailty within the
church, God wants us to worship and praise Him to
discover more about Him. Whether to attend worship
services should not be a decision we make on Saturday
evening or Sunday morning, nor should it be a mere
weekend entertainment destination. Worship is a way
of life, and like forgiveness, it is an attitude. True growth
(for the church and for all of us) is from the inside out.

God is in our midst within the reconciling community of the church. To be a part of this atmosphere is one
of the highest experiences a person could ever hope for.
We need people to talk to. We need fellowship. Silence
about grace is a subtle form of cruelty. I needed the
church, but never realized that the church needed me.

God's love is best revealed through the power of
community—one body of the same substance. We belong

to each other through Christ. A gracious church is our identifying niche where we accept one another because we know God has accepted us. The church is the formal fellowship of the broken and accepted. Once I accepted Christ into my heart, I was instantly made a charter member of the divine and royal family. 1 Peter 2:9 states, "But you are a chosen people, a royal priesthood, a holy nation, a people belonging to God, that you may declare the praises of him who called you out of darkness into his wonderful light."

Through people, I began to discover what "In Christ" and the "Body of Christ" really meant. The state hospital chaplain and his secretary will never know how much their kindness and hospitality influenced my recovery. If two people ever had their acts together, they did. God spoke through these fine servants on several occasions as they answered many of my questions. They were very gifted and seasoned, especially in that setting.

As I continued to read the Bible, I discovered that every person is created in the image of God. The least and worst individual among us is nearer an image of God than the best picture my imagination could ever create. I began to identify with Jesus by being genuine. Throughout the Bible, God shows a marked preference for genuine people over "good" people. For some people, it is very difficult to get real.

Although we all wear a mask, and at times we may need to, it can be a product of shameful compulsive behavior. Someone has said, "We wear masks, and with practice we do it better and better, and they serve us well—except that it gets very lonely because inside the mask is a person who both longs to be known and fears to be known."[1] The church should be a safe haven where we can take our masks off; accordingly, church leaders should be the first people to risk owning up to their needed areas of growth through appropriate self-disclosure.

Christ's Body is where I would find my sense of belonging. The church was created for us to find a sense of unity in His Spirit. The care and love we share on earth originate in the world of the Spirit. James Mayfield states: "The reality of our (inter)dependence on one another is just as powerful as the counter reality of our basic aloneness or independence. We need to accept both our independence and our need for community in order to be whole."[2]

The Communion of Saints

"I pray also that the eyes of your heart may be enlightened in order that you may know the hope to which he has called you, the riches of his glorious inheritance in the saints."

Ephesians 1:18

Community is best illustrated by partaking of the elements of Holy Communion. Because communion is an act of sharing and receiving the sacraments, it is an intimate fellowship. The sacraments themselves are channels of His grace. Communion is also an opportunity to taste and touch sacrifice and forgiveness. Communion was originally two words, common and union, which were combined. This translates from the Greek word *koinonia*, defined as, "the using of a thing in common." Communion is where I celebrate the fact that God poured out His grace upon my guilt. Communion needs to be a slow and gentle process where I reflect on what God has done for me and why He's done it. Then I can leave the communion table with praise and gratitude because of my redemption.

Applying Grace

By now, after three months at the hospital and several weeks of counseling and reading, I was beginning to discover and understand grace. It finally struck me; I had worked all my life to get what could not be earned. I also discovered that when I finally allowed God's grace to lead me, it wasn't a moment of arrival, but rather a moment of departure from a previous life. Although grace did not exempt me from accountability, it empowered me to try to be holy. I needed to pursue holiness before happiness because happiness was a by-product of the former. Happiness depends on what happens to me, externals that I can't always control. Joy is an internal word that is directly related to relationships, not circumstances or happenings. David Seamands points out, "Joy is the inner calm at the eye of the storm; feelings can be stormy, but there can also be an inner sense of rightness to the will of God."[3] Holiness and joy are permanent companions, glued together by His grace. Grace is a product of walking in God's will.

The more I learned about grace, the more I realized my own level of ignorance. In the words of Spurgeon, "I only know more of the extent of what I do not know." Grace changed me, and the difference was not necessarily in what I did, but in why I did it. With grace, I began to experience freedom for my captive spirit. One's spirit need not remain a prisoner of war when grace is an option. God has made it so easy for us. I needed to ask myself: "How can I continue to be burdened with guilt and shame when I believe that I have truly received God's grace?" Grace is sovereign before, during, and after my adversities and joys. Clearly, I had no idea how rich a heritage I inherited. Accepting grace restored my spiritual vision so I could begin to look forward. Isn't it grand to be born twice?

Dr. Ellsworth Kalas writes, "The root problem for 'good' people is not simply that they have a holier-than-thou attitude, but rather a holier-than-God attitude.

They condemn in judgment those whom God does not,
and they refuse to give room to the grace of God—to
others or themselves. For others, because they don't
believe they deserve it; for themselves, because they
don't believe they need it."[4] It was clear that because of
His grace, I was forgiven by the only One who could
condemn me. Now, it was becoming quite obvious that
I was responsible in appropriating grace in order to
forgive myself, my most daunting task of all.

- 12 -

UNDERSTANDING AND EMBRACING FORGIVENESS

"In Him we have redemption through his blood, the forgiveness of sins, in accordance with the riches of God's grace."

Ephesians 1:7

Looking back I realized that although I had been a Christian, I still didn't understand all of the dynamics of forgiveness. I thought I was well versed on the topic, when in reality all I had was a very shallow knowledge. For years, I was perpetually stuck on the notion that although God had forgiven me, I hadn't forgiven myself. I needed to go back and re-examine the most powerful and misunderstood dynamic of God's love. First, I needed to look at forgiveness from a general perspective.

Forgiveness, like grace, is the willingness to see a situation or person from a much higher (Godly) perspective. Forgiveness and grace are eternally intertwined. If grace happens, so does forgiveness. Because of grace, one is motivated to forgive. The word "forgiven" means "to lift off, to carry away." The word "forgive" in the English language is "an extended, expanded, strengthened form of the verb 'to give.' It is giving at its deepest level, of self-giving, of giving forth and giving up deeply held parts of the self."[1] The only sense of redemption from not being able to undo what we have done is through forgiveness.

God's forgiveness is a state of reckoning, which includes total exoneration and vindication. When we are forgiven by God, we are eternally justified. While God's forgiveness is instantaneous (in fact, but not necessarily feeling), our forgiveness of others or ourselves can take a much longer time. *Feeling* forgiven is not essential for the reality of it. God wants to forgive us but often we are reluctant to be open to receive His forgiveness.

In grace and forgiveness, Jesus was not necessarily interested in what I had done wrong once I had repented. Repentance means "to change," "to turn around" in behavior and thought. When someone is genuinely sorry, the behavior stops and there is no need for token apologies, which are usually meant for the benefit of self rather than the injured party. Repeated apologies in response to repetitive behavior can often become cheap insults.

Forgiveness invites bold change. The deliberate process of forgiveness is to cease the feelings of resentment against an offender and can be very strenuous and complicated. In forgiveness, we give up our claim for requital by allowing room for error, selfishness, or weakness. Sir Francis Bacon wrote, "We read that we ought to forgive our enemies, but we do not read that we ought to forgive our (family) or friends."

The Ministry of Reconciliation

> "All this is from God, who reconciled us to himself through Christ and gave us the ministry of reconciliation: that God was reconciling the world to himself in Christ, not counting men's sins against them."
>
> II Corinthians 5:18-19

Forgiveness is a one-way process and is unconditional on another's response. Our forgiveness may be of no value to the person we are forgiving. Reconciliation, on the other hand, is a two-way process. Thus, we are not solely responsible for reconciliation. We can offer it, but unlike forgiveness, reconciliation must be contingent upon the other person genuinely owning their mistakes and being willing to move forward. In reconciliation, the offended and the offender need each other. When we reconcile, we accept something unpleasant. Reconciliation restores to harmonious friendship. The Greek word for reconcile means "to render something otherwise."

Forgiveness can eventually take place, but it doesn't necessarily reconcile us back into a personal relationship, especially if one did not exist before the offense. Many people use forgiveness as a misguided way of controlling someone by having nothing to do with him after the fact. But forgiveness should never be a means to distance or to rid ourselves of a relationship. We forgive in the sight of Christ (II Corinthians 2:10).

Through Christ's death on the cross, God forgave everyone, but not everyone is reconciled to Him, because He made His will dependent on our choice(s). We are encouraged to have a personal relationship with each other (after the fact), but we are not necessarily bound or obligated. If a personal relationship (such as a marriage) did exist before the offense, reconciliation should be an all-exhaustive goal for both parties. We don't bring reconciliation about on our own; it is God who ultimately reconciles. In forgiveness, we are indirectly reconciled together in a relationship as fallen human beings.

Boundaries

> "Forgiveness creates boundaries, for it gets bad debt off of your property."
>
> Henry Cloud and John Townsend

We forgive people because both parties need it. The walls that surround us are broken down in order to reestablish new and healthy boundaries. Reconciliation, if possible, may take much longer than forgiveness. There is no need to rush. We can use Hannah Whitehall Smith's famous phrase when we pray "the prayer of relinquishment," leaving the timing and future applications in God's hands. Forgiveness doesn't remove boundaries, limits, or consequences. It does increase their value and meaning. Formal justice is when the offender pays his debt. Forgiveness is when the offended pays. Bishop Stephen Neill writes, "Forgiveness recognizes the wrongdoer as a person, but there is a special need for help that can be rendered only by the one to whom the wrong was done. Forgiveness springs from a self-forgetfulness that is more concerned about another's well-being than about its own."[2]

Boundaries are permeable and flexible, but walls are solid and rigid. One's wall needs to be respected, for without it the person may not have survived. But a wall can begin to outlive its functional usefulness and cause more harm than good. Boundaries, on the other hand, help us take control of our lives by signaling when to say yes or no. Boundaries define our areas of responsibility, creating a mutual balance. "Inside the protective boundaries is the whole person. The conscious self is where the adult part of us operates; it is primarily cognitive. The unconscious part is where the feelings and memories of the inner child are stored," according to Earl Henslin.[3]

To forgive means we will never receive what was owed us. When we forgive, we begin to grieve what we didn't receive. Forgiveness promotes our boundaries when we appropriately or temporarily detach and disengage from the person (behavior) who has hurt us. This skillful and loving process is still possible and many times needed within the whole realm of forgiveness. The relationship still exists, but it is now more specifically defined. Creating good boundaries means being close enough to feel connected, yet distant enough to be objective.

After much study I have learned that often it is our low self-esteem that prevents us from forgiving someone who has hurt us. We may feel morally superior to a person as long as we don't forgive him, because we feel we have something on him. This is our form of leverage over the person (event) by being able to stand over him, physically and/or psychologically, and talk at him with a condescending attitude or tone of voice. We may reason that the person has not even asked for forgiveness, much less does he deserve it. This is irrelevant. The person we haven't forgiven is most likely the very person who is emotionally controlling us.

We need to give up our self-imposed control and relinquish "our rights" to God's domain. At the time, giving up control was one of the most difficult things I had ever done. More importantly, in the years to come, I would learn that giving up control would be a daily struggle.

Genuine forgiveness is the dethroning of self, particularly our rights, titles, and claims. As Christians, we do not have a bill of rights. When we refuse to forgive others or ourselves, we show that God's forgiveness has not penetrated the depths of our soul. When we forgive, we (God and you) bear the pain and absorb the hurt. The more forgiveness we incorporate into our lives, the less compulsive behavior we will have.

When I refused to forgive myself, God patiently stood to the side and let me contend with my issues alone. This was my consequence for defiantly refusing to do it His way. He simply honored my choice, although He certainly didn't agree with it. It takes a great amount of courage to forgive. Refusing to forgive is the destruction of joy. H.R. Macintosh tells us, "In every great forgiveness there is enshrined a great agony."

The greatest weakness Satan loves to see in us is our unwillingness to forgive. When we forgive, we give all the responsibility to God and, simultaneously, remove Satan from the picture, or at least keep him at bay. We let go of the injustice and become free to live our own lives. Forgiveness, like grace, does not take one's accountability away. Nor does it mean we simply tolerate injustice. Unfruitful deeds of the darkness should be exposed (Ephesians 5:11). By holding people accountable, such as having them arrested for a crime, we are actually extending grace to them by offering them a chance to face the truth. David Augsburger remarks:

> "Accepting and forgiving are different processes. We accept persons for the good that they are or do. We forgive persons for the evil that they did or caused.
>
> Excusing and forgiving are different processes. We excuse people when we no longer hold them accountable. We forgive people when we hold them accountable but do not excuse.

Tolerating and forgiving are different processes. We tolerate what another has done when we overlook or ignore. We forgive what we cannot tolerate, and will not overlook, or ignore.
Forgetting and forgiving are different processes. We do not need to forgive if we can simply forget—forgetting is passive, avoidant, repressive; it denies, detaches, dismisses. We do not forget when we forgive, but the meaning of the memory changes—forgiving is active and aware; it is recognizing the injury, owning the pain, and reaching out to reframe, re-create, restore, reconstruct, rebuild, reopen what can be opened."[4]

The person we haven't forgiven may have been deceased for years. Or we may have been dead (spiritually) during the time we weren't in the process of forgiving. We have been dead in the sense that we have been living and thinking in the past rather than in the present. Many dead people control from their graves and the living party is not aware of it. Death can make the control more subtle and stronger because people may no longer feel they can confront the person. Confrontation is still possible, although through more indirect means. Many people visit cemeteries in order to be released from their oppressive pasts. Cemetery trips are emotionally symbolic, but they offer many tangibles, such as time, solitude, reflection, and the living power of memories. Life-changing decisions are often made in cemeteries. As Christians, the greatest news we have ever heard came from a graveyard!

Writing letters to the deceased can be extremely helpful. The letter may never be read and one can do with it whatever is desired such as sealing, burning, shredding, or continuing to add to it as a personal journal. In this exercise, the writer has seized all of the appropriate control.

One of the most spiritually rewarding things I have ever done was to write my father a letter a few months after his death. To this day, I've kept the sealed letter in my desk drawer at work.

On the other hand, I've never felt the need to write Tina. Maybe a part of me felt she was there the whole time and already knew the details of what happened that night, not to mention my feelings toward her. More likely, I've had no idea where to begin.

When trying to come to terms with our past, a good question to ask ourselves is: Who or what has the power in my heart (home)?

If a home is plagued by emotional turmoil and chaos, it can be indirectly caused by a person who has hurt us many years ago. Although forgiveness can't change the past, it can mark a refreshing new start and future. If we hate a person, we are actually giving them power over our heart and attitude. Don't dignify a person's inappropriate behavior by hating him. Refuse to let this person or event beat you. Reclaim God's power and freedom through forgiveness. Make the person's behavior as irrelevant and insignificant in your present-day self as much as possible. Settling old scores only rekindles the fire of hate. In forgiveness, we confront our hatred. Forgiveness will allow us to find something far greater than our heartache. Ephesians 4:32 commands us: "Be kind and compassionate to one another, forgiving each other, just as in Christ God forgave you."

We need to join and connect with others as we commit to enter the forgiveness process. Jesus wants us to move forward, through and past the hurt into an attitude and lifestyle of forgiveness. Forgiveness is the delicate fusion of our wounds and healing. But it was very difficult for me to expose all of my wounds in order to begin and continue the healing process. At the first twinge of trouble, I had a tendency to run, although I had no clue where or to whom I was running. At that time, the act of fleeing was more important than the destination.

Healing does not come by removing the defense, but by actually moving closer to the defender. The bigger and deeper the wound, generally the longer it will take for healing to occur. Forgiveness is born in sorrow. "Will you forgive me?" and "I forgive you" will be the most important question and statement we will ever make. Forgiveness affects all of our relationships.

One example of post-death forgiveness is a middle-aged woman who had been sexually abused by her father over thirty years ago. He had been dead for years, but the woman was still emotionally under the dominating reign of his curse. Although she did not formally report the abuse for various reasons, her counselor simply asked how she felt about reporting him now. After an incredulous look and some conversation, she decided to do so and went to the police station and filed a report. The police realized what she therapeutically needed to do and graciously accepted her statement. The woman felt better than she had in years. By holding her father accountable, it was easier for her to begin the process of forgiving him. God worked through several people in her life: the police, the counselor(s), and others. The woman had finally allowed other people to help her. More importantly, this also helped with her more pressing issue, the need to confront herself.

We need to do all we can to reclaim our boundaries and dignity which were damaged by an invader or predator. But the overall results aren't in our hands.

What the police did with her statement (their response) and the fact the father had died was irrelevant. One word of caution: people can resolve similar issues without necessarily reporting them. In many states there is no statute of limitations on reporting an offense such as rape. Reporting a crime is one example of reclaiming a part of ourselves; it also helps to prevent the crime from recurring. Although we may encourage one to report, we need to respect the decision of the harmed person. It is ultimately their call to make.

The Value of Scars

> "Peace be with you! After he said this, he showed them his hands and side. The disciples were overjoyed when they saw the Lord."
>
> John 20:19-20

Although we may have started the process of forgiveness, we can still have remnants of anger and emotional scarring. Forgiveness did not remove the physical consequences of my father's drinking, nor did it remove the emotional consequences of my actions. Even after the Resurrection, Jesus bore the scars from His wounds. Jesus valued His scars so much He decided to keep them when He could have easily erased them. He used His scars as a way to identify Himself to any unbelievers or doubters (John 20:20-29). His eternal scars are now key components of His healing process. Scars and wounds can be enriched to give authenticity to the victories over our struggles. Although scars may represent an ugly side of our lives, they can illustrate our victory and endurance. I used to hide the scars on my arm because I was so self-conscious and did not want to have to explain how they got there.

Jesus' scars represented the dark and gruesome side of Calvary, but they also symbolized victory over physical and emotional death. His scars reminded me that death is not the end, but the beginning. Scars are not necessarily open wounds, and they can increase how we value our inner and spiritual experiences. Many times, because of our outward scars, we begin to explore our inner substance. If we can look beyond or through the pain of our scars, we can experience God's goodness as He continues to shower us with His mighty grace.

The Diseased Condition of Victimization

"Forgiveness strikes a blow at the root of one's victim status," writes Stephen Seamands.[5] The victim needs to realize he does have an identity apart from the pain. It took me many years to discover this point. Only by accepting the death of my worldly identity could I move away from the victim role and find my spiritual and emotional identity. According to E. Stanley Jones, "One does not know who he is until he knows whose he is."

People who choose to remain emotional victims actually *need* aggressors to oppress them. People who adopt the victim role can eventually become victimizers, too. When we refuse to forgive others or ourselves, we are victimizing God by hurting and offending Him with our pride. Pride was my form of spiritual cancer.

Many people are truly victimized by things out of their control. This cold, harsh fact should never be minimized; we need to have empathy, understanding, compassion, and an attentive ear for each victim, and for their victimizer(s). What we can change is whether or not we are to remain emotional victims.

Victim-like thinking, a common cognitive distortion, is a form of defensiveness in which the victim becomes justified where he is. In my mind, I was justified because of the overall sense of unfairness I felt. Victims are often raised by or live with devoted rescuers as they continue to carry their emotional burdens. As a result, old beliefs or perceptions continue to impede their lives. It takes daring boldness to challenge these false beliefs, and for one to take responsibility for his life. In part, one may have to admit mistakes in certain aspects of his rationale following a traumatic event(s). And that was something I simply hated and refused to do. My stubbornness was getting the best of me.

Victims often contend the only wrongdoing or transgression is what the victimizer did to him. Their (the victim's) plight is based solely on another. Sustaining their victim role gives them an excuse outside of their own responsibility to themselves to blame for their troubles.

Bitterness can be as difficult to escape from as Alcatraz. The somber fact remains that many people do not want deliverance from behind the bars of bitterness. They have become blinded by them and don't see or want any other choices. In bitterness, we focus on the person who has hurt us or on ourselves rather than on God. Victims think they save face or settle some meaningless score by blaming the world and closing the vault to their hearts. As C.S. Lewis tells us, "We are half-hearted creatures fooling around with drink and sex and ambition when infinite joy is offered us, like an ignorant child who wants to go on making mud pies in a slum because he cannot imagine what is meant by the offer of a holiday at sea. We are far too easily pleased."[6]

When we think solely of ourselves as victims of others' behavior, we deny the reality that we are actually a victim of ourselves. Over the years, we can emotionally abuse ourselves more than any of our abusers combined. Similarly, when self-imposed victims encounter Christ, they discover they are the offenders, not the offended. When we choose to not forgive others or ourselves, we choose to remain a victim duped by our own ignorance. We also decide to continue our internal skirmish and the outbreak of our bitterness infection. We will never be asked to give anyone more grace or forgiveness than God has already freely given us. And as long as someone else is responsible for your behavior, you will never get better. My problem was that I thought God was responsible for my behavior. The words of Eleanor Roosevelt, "No one can make you feel less about yourself without your consent" would become very meaningful to me.

According to Robert Schreiter, "The question should not be 'How can I bring myself, as a victim, to forgive those who have violated me....?' It should be, rather, 'How can I discover the mercy of God welling up in my own life, and where does that lead me?'"[7] Forgiveness is a process in which we discover we are more like the people who have hurt us, rather than that we differ from them. There is a very thin line between the best and the worst of us. In the compelling and vibrant energy of forgiveness, our focus gradually begins to turn to others and away from ourselves.

Often we take things too personally. Others' inappropriate behavior is not necessarily about us. It is just a form of imposing or interpreting their distorted perceptions onto us. It is simply their way of seeing their deluded world. Taking things too personally can be a form of subtle selfishness on our part, if we are excessively concerned about others' behavior toward us.

Virgil Elizonda states, "The greatest damage of an offense—often greater than the offense itself—is that it destroys my freedom to be me. I hate the offender for what he has done to me but in the very hatred I allow him to become the Lord and Master of my life."[8] Forgiveness is the only antidote for the toxin of resentment.

An unknown author once wrote, "Forgiveness is an unreasonable behavior—against our human nature of getting even. It defies our logic and common sense; all the more reason why Christ came to show us the benefits of forgiveness. For those who choose not to forgive, they will find themselves in a state of spiritual paralysis—still under the control of the offender rather than God himself. An 'eye for an eye' approach leaves everyone blind."[9]

Warped Presumptions

Through invaluable counseling at the hospital, I learned how many unrealistic, unconscious demands I had made on myself. To some limited extent, it began as an overcompensation for trying to please my father as a child. My father modeled a flawed authority figure which, in turn, helped fuel a number of defective concepts on my part. Yet I was responsible for becoming aware of and for changing those faulty concepts.

Because dysfunctional backgrounds can breed "super responsibility" in behavior and thought, even the most petty act(s) noticed by anyone perceived to be in authority is a basis for a lingering sense of guilt and shame. Notwithstanding my background, there obviously would have been guilt over the accident, but my past was a significant factor in the total depth and scope of guilt. I had created an "inner critic" in order to "protect" myself from external criticism well before crashing into that oak tree. But my issue wasn't a tree; it was the cross, an altogether different form of a tree. I finally discovered I had been under the looming shadow of the wrong tree. "For a tree is recognized by its fruit" (Matthew 12:33).

I needed to confront my internal irrationalities and develop a more rational and flexible conscience. In short,

I needed to develop an appropriate attitude toward failure. Failures framed in a positive light are merely second chances to get it right. Learning from my mistakes increased my awareness of God and His grace. Someone once said, "Learning to live with failure(s) is a sign of spiritual and emotional maturity. Rather than being totally crushed by failure, the mature person learns from his mistakes and moves away from them, not putting too much pressure on himself that he always succeed."[10] We then become less threatened by our past and future mistakes. I had always viewed my mistakes as confirmation of my low self-esteen. This is quite evident in my first conscious thought after the car's impact on the tree, "What have I done now?"

Mistakes can bring us to places we normally would have avoided. Fritz Perls tells us that we shouldn't live in fear because of our mistakes. Mistakes are not necessarily sins. Our mistakes are often creative ways of performing certain tasks, and they can be a form of our ingenuity. Mistakes can symbolize our courage to give of ourselves.

One of the most difficult leg(s) of our spiritual pilgrimage toward wholeness is going back to the place where we made the mistake. But this time we are not alone. God is a God of second, third, fourth, etc., chances. He will do whatever it takes to help us get it right; we will never wear out our welcome with Him.

The Need for Others in Healing the Heartache(s)

God, in His common grace, was speaking to me through the hospital staff, but more so through the patients. One friend I met survived a house fire, which killed the rest of his family. Once the fire started, his first instinct was to get out, which he did. But in doing so, he was unable to save the others. His survivor guilt outweighed his enormous grief. Another woman had accidentally run over her toddler when backing her car up on the driveway. Responsibility can be so stern when compared to intentions. These two people were just some of the many distressed and grieving souls who had experienced horrific traumas. And I thought I had it tough. Their tears of sorrow actually helped heal my wounds.

In a paradoxical way, the patients enabled me to realize how thankful I was for the many things God provided that I had taken for granted. Their experiences had an overwhelming impact on my heart, giving me a sense of connectedness most people thankfully can't offer. In essence, we embraced each others' wounds. A renewed sense of belonging and vibrant energy had begun to grow in me. We fed off each other through our experiences and rallied around and upon each other.

Solitude

"The present state of the world is diseased. If I were asked for my advice, I should reply, 'Create silence.' Jesus' ministry grew out of concentrated silence. He was sustained through the demands and stress by that custom of His, those frequent all-night retreats into silence."

Soren Kierkegaard

Solitude would be another key factor in my emotional recovery. Getting away from it all for an extended period of time gave me the time and space to identify and reflect upon all of my feelings without the interruptions of the daily stresses of life. Solitude allowed me to receive and maintain a healthier, holier perspective. I needed to create places and times of purpose in the world of transition and rush. Henri Nouwen tells us, "Silence not only teaches us to listen, but it also teaches us to speak."

Previously, silence was somewhat threatening to me because I emotionally related it to loneliness, emptiness, and despair. I gravitated to "clutter" for a sense of companionship, not realizing the clutter was hindering my spiritual growth. I would need to simplify my life by taking many things off my plate and by becoming more selective of what I placed on it.

We may be addicted to the frenzy of rushing because it feeds our insecurities by giving us a false sense of importance, temporarily filling voids within us. It also delays the inevitable of looking within ourselves to find what our issues really are. Only the consistent discipline of solitude can help break our rush addiction. We need to heed Jesus' words to his disciples, "'Come with me by yourselves to a quiet place and get some rest.' So they went away by themselves in a boat to a solitary place" (Mark 6:31-32).

Solitude suggests being removed or apart from others, though not inaccessible. It is being alone, although not lonely. It is also a passive form of searching, born out of a robust hunger. Solitude approaches the situation, while isolation avoids it. Solitude leads us to conversion in which the self dies because of our focus on God. In solitude, we ultimately move closer to God and people.

Thankfully, we need not go to the extreme of a state hospital setting to find solitude. The state hospital was an indirect result, because I didn't prioritize or incorporate solitude within my lifestyle. We can easily permit the world to dictate our agenda and allow the subtle erosion of our values. Henri Nouwen suggests, "In solitude we become compassionate people, deeply aware of our solidarity in brokenness with all humanity and ready to reach out to anyone in need. It is the place where Christ remodels us in His own image and frees us from the victimizing compulsions of the world."[11]

Isolation, on the other hand, can be a form of avoidance, for it emphasizes total detachment. The isolating nature of false guilt and toxic shame makes us less likely to deal with it in a functional manner. Similarly, the process of forgiveness is not a solitary transaction between you and God. My sights and scope had been set too low, and I didn't even bother to look to or for other people. In my early childhood and even after becoming a Christian, when I thought of God, He was often a solitary figure. But by expanding my scope and vision, I learned the internal process of forgiveness is actually more external. All the answers are not within me and no amount of self-searching will change the outcome. I would need to think outside of myself most of the time. This would be tougher to do because of my introverted personality.

- 13 -

CONFRONTING OURSELVES
AT THE CROSS

"And anyone who does not take his cross and
follow me is not worthy of me."
Matthew 10:38

Confrontation is a face-to-face meeting designed to
be a challenging, refining, and uplifting encounter. I
mistakenly viewed it strictly as a battle that someone
(most likely me) was going to lose. Although we need to
gently approach others at the appropriate time, we also
need to be mature enough to welcome being approached.
To draw near or to confront is a positive process that
many people have given a negative connotation. It is a
comparison of ideas which helps bring things into
meaningful purpose. Jesus lovingly confronted people
at every encounter. Jesus came to confront. We need to
invite and welcome confrontation in order to have a
face-to-face encounter between guilt, shame, grace and
forgiveness.

The cross sheds light on our wounds, giving us a new perspective from which to see them. Stephen Seamands states, "Reframed with wood from Calvary's cross, our painful memory pictures look different. The cross reveals to us that for the complex problem of evil and suffering, there is no simplistic quick fix of restoration and healing—even for God Himself. Deep wounds require deep healing."[1] At the cross, we can reflect on our wounds in the Light of His. By embracing His stripes, we are to rely on His wounds to find comfort for ours. Isaiah 53:5 says, "...and by His wounds we are healed."

At the cross, God's opinion of me was truly revealed. When I was at my worst, it demonstrated God's love for me in the most profound way. Through the cross, God also disclosed the deadliness of my sins of self-love and false idols. The cross also shows God's solidarity with you and me. The deepest meaning of the cross is the suffering of God and how it relates to us. Things of this world caused both His suffering and mine. But only the things of His world are the instruments by which I could find redemption and healing from such suffering. The high cost of forgiveness is the cross. As Frank Lake writes, "...He bore the dreadful limits of redemptive identification. Neither the anxiety of commitment He experienced in Gethsemane, which made His sweat like drops of blood fall to the ground, nor the anxiety of separation in the final dereliction, diverted Him for one moment from His path of obedient redemptive suffering."[2]

Connecting with God

The continued regimen of counseling, reading, prayer, silence, and listening to Christian music began to take root within my spirit. After five humbling months within the confines of the hospital grounds, some of my new perception(s) and understanding of grace and forgiveness had grown enough for me to have the confidence to be formally released. Was I completely healed or recovered? No, but I was pointed in the the right direction by God's loving compass. My supply of resources had been dramatically overhauled, too. Many new insights enlightened me to what my affliction had brought me, and I was now willing to let go and move on. I had to question myself, just as Jesus questioned the man who had been (emotionally?) crippled for 38 years, "Do you want to get well" (John 5:6)?

After a long period of suffering, many people lose the fight to get better. Consider this man who suffered over 38 years; he hadn't convinced Christ he really wanted to be healed. Jesus' pointed question to the man lets us know how well He really knows us.

Don't assume all people want to be healed. Many refuse to do the necessary work or experience the appropriate pain for healing to occur. Successful living illustrates the necessity of continuous adjusting and evolving. The only constant in our lives, other than Christ, is change. But change is a threat to some of our hallowed ruts. Many people become emotional dropouts when they refuse to confront the pain of their earlier years. They enshrine their hurt and unresolved issues and grant them holy and sacred status. I teetered here for what turned out to be years.

First, an old wound needs to be cleaned, because cleansing begins the healing process. Reshaping or remodeling our hearts and minds does not always feel good. Making peace is a very painful process. Rather than adjusting to be healed, many people merely adapt to the suffering of stagnation. We have a tendency to grow comfortable with our misery. I know I did. Comfort zones can be dire opponents of change. Obviously, not all people who struggle have these issues. Many people do have the mettle to get well and their resolute spirit is one of the greatest manifestations of the power of Christ. God is all about radically changed lives.

Another factor inhibiting my recovery included the fear of change, even positive change. The unknown is inundated with anxiety. With positive transition came more responsibility, and I wasn't too keen on that idea. But it is in change that we ultimately find peace. Because of my previous refusal to trust, I wasn't convinced that change would be best for me. I also wanted to be the great negotiator or agent (rather than God) in trying to come to the terms of my own spiritual contract extension, but I discovered my bargaining chips were worthless. And, if I were to fail in life, this tragedy would be a great excuse I could always rely on.

Earlier, because of the guilt and shame, a part of me felt I didn't deserve to get better. But now I understood through God's grace and forgiveness, He wanted to give me what I didn't deserve. God has nothing to do with what we deserve, but He has everything to do with what we don't deserve. I also had a fear of forgiving myself, and had clung to the fear as if it had value. Fear had more value than the feelings of emptiness or help-lessness. I needed to move beyond fear to faith in order to be free, just as I needed to move from blame to belief.

The Verdict is In

"Many seek an audience with a ruler, but it is from the Lord that man gets justice."   •

Proverbs 29:26

Humanity was actually on trial and the verdict has been reached. We are guilty on all counts. But because of

Christ, there is no death penalty, jail time, or even probation. The moment we trust Christ, we are given immunity from eternal punishment, and our issue is settled. Jesus, as the unassuming servant, washes the dirtiest and vilest parts of our heart, mind, and feet. He only hopes our walk will be one of gratitude. More than anything, God yearns for us to have a grateful heart rather than a burdened one. Effective prayers are spurred by grateful thoughts. Corrie ten Boom writes that God throws our past into His sea of forgetfulness and posts a sign, "NO FISHING ALLOWED."[3]

We have a tendency to be so historical! The most neglected doctrine of theology is God's forgetfulness. The judgment of our sin was laid on His Son and as in our legal courts, there is no double jeopardy. But we need to trust God, not merely try Him. But like salvation, trust may not immediately ease our suffering. That was a tough lesson for me to learn, too. Many dynamics of trust can be painstakingly slow. This is where patience may be our most valuable asset. We trust as we heal. Trust, like hope, is a wholesome form of dependence on the future. Trust is an assured reliance on the sufficiency of Christ. When we trust in God, our confidence is placed in Him. The substance of trust is found in Jesus' words upon the cross, "Father, into your hands I commit my spirit" (Luke 23:46).

If we continue to put ourselves on trial by not forgiving ourselves or others, we are inadvertently competing with Christ's finest moments on the cross; we are not giving full meaning to the Crucifixion. It is all in vain, as we choose to carry our body of death with us. The foot of the cross is the only place to unburden ourselves of emotional baggage and receive all the necessities for freedom.

Our emotional baggage only ensures long guilt trips that go nowhere. We need to book the trip elsewhere and learn the art of traveling light and receive His everlasting joy! His forgiveness is final and not just until our next inevitable sin. Once our mind, heart and soul grasp the magnitude of His forgiveness, we, too, can sing out, "Whom the Son sets free is free indeed" (John 8:36)!

Forgiving Myself

It had taken many painstaking years and the experiences of those wonderful people within the hospital for me to learn that when I chose not to forgive myself after God had already done so, I was giving myself higher standards of forgiveness than God. I had been playing God and did not even realize it. This was the moment I got up from my chair in the library, and walked and literally stumbled to the altar within the chapel. On my knees, I began to weep and wept for what felt like years. These were the moments when my tears were eternally transformed from tears of guilt and shame to tears of indescribable joy.

Joyful tears originate in our sorrow. God seeks our tears in order to bless them, for our tears belong to Him. Our transformed tears create our sustained joy. Spurgeon says that tears are liquid prayers. I must have prayed more than I realized. Washington Irving writes, "There is a sacredness in tears. They are not the mark of weakness, but of power. They are the messengers of overwhelming grief, of deep contrition and of unspeakable love."[4]

The first place I ever experienced true peace was within the walls of the hospital's chapel. Now finally through my obstinacy, I had come to the end of myself and arrived at the point of surrender. I came up from my knees with an overwhelming sense of gratitude. For the first time in my life, I rose as a man, forgiven by his

Father. A.W. Tozer explains the experience of crucifying the self like this: "The man on the cross is facing in only one direction. He is not going back, and he has no further plans of his own."[5] Surrendering is giving up, but not giving in. For me, it was giving up my need for the cancer of control. The self must die before we can carry His cross with effectiveness. Denying the self is not denying our self-worth but our self-will. The process of getting to the end of ourselves is a very exhausting trip. Likewise, the slow walk up to Calvary is very steep.

As an evolving Christian, I began to be self-aware enough to know the times when I spoke or acted in ways which separated me from God, other people, and from my true self; it caused me to experience righteous guilt. But this newly formed sensitivity needed to be tempered with rationality and sensibility. In the car accident, I made an instantaneous and unintentional mistake, the same mistake millions of people have made, although the vast majority will not have such a deadly outcome. Facing real, righteous guilt, Christ gave me the necessary courage to exercise moral and spiritual integrity by taking responsibility for my conduct. In short, I needed to become accountable for my behavior without beating myself up. In the past, it was very difficult for me to distinguish the difference between the two.

In forgiving myself, I could see myself through God's eyes for the first time, rather than through my guilt and shame laden vision. I would still need to continue to saturate myself in Scripture and fellowship in order to create and sustain new thought and behavioral patterns. Getting to the end of myself would be an on-going venture. I also needed to "forgive" God for allowing the adversity to occur. Theologically, it is obvious God had done nothing for which to be forgiven. We don't forgive God because He needs it; rather we forgive Him because we need it. Forgiveness in this context simply means letting go of any anger, disappointment, and hurt we may feel toward Him.

Forgiving myself brought the discovery for which I had been searching. It provided me with a sense of inner peace and joy beyond my imagination. When I forgave myself, I lost myself in the awe and grandeur of God. Forgiving myself created a cease-fire for the civil war within me, and it created a liberating freedom of my energies by turning inner restlessness into peace. Forgiving myself allowed me the freedom to be myself; it was a standing offer (and acceptance) to live life in the moment—no longer in the past. It also gave me a rejuvenated zest for life. Deuteronomy 30:19-20 tells us, "Now choose life, so that you and your children may live and that you may love the Lord your God, listen to his voice, and hold fast to him."

The more at peace I was with myself, the more likely I was to get along with others. When I refused to forgive myself, I didn't possess the necessary humility to face myself as I really was. I missed out on priceless joy by being too harsh and judgmental. I discovered that forgiving myself was a bold choice of stepping into power.

Needing to channel and reconstruct my stubbornness toward a vitality of life, I was finally determined not to allow this tragedy to beat me. The decision to forgive myself began a life-long process of moving from self-imposed victim to victor (a survivor) in Christ. I also realized another dynamic concerning the act of forgiving myself. I couldn't forgive myself any more than I could save myself. Salvation and forgiveness are rooted in His grace alone. They are divine acts. Even the term "forgiving yourself" still whiffs too much of I or me. Forgiving oneself is more of a discovery of the completeness and wholeness of God's forgiveness. In other words, if you really believe God forgives you, the process of forgiving yourself actually becomes moot. When I claimed I hadn't forgiven myself, I was undermining the richness and fullness of God's grace and forgiveness. Forgiving myself was a grace and God process, although it still involved a conscious choice on my part.

Many of our biblical leaders had to ask for forgiveness in order to move into the ministry God had planned for them. Jonah, who actually attempted to outrun God, was still used in a great and powerful revival. David had a future after experiencing the shame of committing adultery. Paul was a persecutor of Christians before he was a leader for them. Zacchaeus was a thief who laundered money. Moses was a murderer, yet in God's time, he would declare the eighth commandment: "You shall not murder" (Exodus 20:13). The woman at the well had to experience forgiveness for her promiscuous past. Each person, just like you and me, had a choice to make as to how they would use their past experiences. God's greatest gift to us is the power of choice.

> "Worldly wisdom knows what distress and weakness and failure are, but it does not know the godlessness of men. It also does not know that man is destroyed only by his sin and can be healed only by forgiveness."[6]
>
> Dietrich Bonhoeffer

On the following page is a brief summary of the steps I took to resolve the false guilt and toxic shame. Please understand this was a very slow process involving many hours of prayer, reading, counseling, anger, tears, and joy. Other than the first step, they are in no particular order and may overlap.

1. Ask God for FORGIVENESS and STRENGTH to forgive yourself (regardless of what present concepts you may have).

2. To IDENTIFY with specificity what you feel guilt and shame about.

3. What was your INTENT? Even though intentions are irrelevant to forgiveness.

4. Is the guilt and shame logical or RATIONAL?

5. Allow a healthy, objective, PASTORAL COUNSELOR to describe your behavior from a non-judgmental and COMPASSIONATE frame of reference.

6. Become AWARE of all your guilt and shame. Asking yourself the question, "What would be examples of how I would speak or act out unconscious guilt or shame?

7. What CAN YOU DO behaviorally that would make you feel better (such as apologize, make amends, pay someone back, etc.)?

8. RELEASE CHILDHOOD BAGGAGE from your family of origin closet.

9. CHANGE FAULTY CONCEPTS of God, guilt, shame, grace and forgiveness.

10. RE-ADJUST STANDARDS AND EXPECTATIONS. Be real and genuine.

11. ALLOW GOD AND PEOPLE TO LOVE YOU.

12. CHOOSE TO USE YOUR EXPERIENCE FOR GOD'S GLORY and His Kingdom (in any vocation or endeavor).

- 14 -

POSITIVE RESPONSES TO ADVERSITY

"When walking through the 'valley of shadows,' remember, a shadow is cast by a Light."

H.K. Barclay

I could sense the momentum building toward my pending release from the hospital. In the meantime, I felt empowered to learn more concerning the dynamics of human suffering. I was eager to explore every aspect of the topic. Specifically, I wanted to learn how it was similar to or different from my personal experience. I was beginning to be intrigued with the thought that maybe one day my experience could be of some benefit to others. I continued to read and study as my fascination with helping others grew.

A person can have peace without understanding and justice. The epitome of peace is when the injustice gives it more value. The Crucifixion, the greatest injustice of all time, became in God's time, our greatest blessing. "The cross is where Jesus identifies with our undeserved suffering, but also our deserved punishment," according to David Seamands.[1] Any injustice in our lives can be eternally offset by the privilege of choosing our fate in the next. Originally, the concept of fairness was pre-ordained when God planted an apple tree. But we chose to run afoul.

Character

Character is the whole of mental and ethical traits marking and individualizing a person. It is a form of moral excellence and firmness. We know adversity builds character, but it also reveals it. Character is our moxie under pressure, which distinguishes us from others. To paraphrase P.C. Craigie: Adversity can test and discipline us. It removes some of the props and supports upon which we depend. It can also cast us back on God who gives us the strength to survive. The severity of the adversity can undermine our superficial dependence of that which is not grounded in God. Adversity makes or breaks a person. It can provide strength, not the strength of self-sufficiency, but the strength that only comes from a personal relationship with God.[2]

Adversity removed the veneer of pretension to reveal the truth of what or who I was. Not to sound insensitive, but God was more concerned about the content of my character than my circumstances. Character is manifested in an unassuming, genuine lifestyle. Pretense merely isolated me from God. Character also frees us from trying to impress people we don't know or even like. Our focus switches from trying to impress people with how good we are, to starting to share how great God is.

"Nearly all men can stand adversity, but if you want to test a man's character, give him power."
Abraham Lincoln

Why?

Rather than focus on the adversity (circumstances), we should ask the only pertinent question, "Lord, what would you have me do now?" In His time, His answer(s) will surely come as we are reminded in Romans 8:28, "And we know that in all things God works for the good of those who love him, who have been called according to his purpose."

In this world, made corrupt by our choices, good and evil are at war. We are sometimes caught in a bewildering and vicious crossfire. In the brutality of war, we should actually expect the harsh reality of unjust suffering. In war, because of so many innocent deaths, there is virtually no morality. No cause can ever hide that fact.

God's gift of human reason gives us the ability and privilege to make choices. Although sovereign, God controls our world in accordance with His self-imposed rules or limits to promote order over chaos. His steadfast dependence on these rules is what gives us the freedom to choose. It is a miracle when He does intervene. The problem arises when we judge His love or our depth of faith on whether or not He intercedes. It will most likely remain a mystery as to why He may or may not intervene. Mysteries never have any satisfactory explanations. Often we hurt ourselves when we insist on a miracle rather than the more likely reality. Reality can be incredibly slow and has no glitz. We do need to pray for and believe a miracle can happen, but we need to realize it may not occur. In spite of suffering, we aren't entitled to miracles. We should heed Proverbs 3:5, "Trust in the Lord with all your heart and lean not on your own understanding."

Many people think everything that occurs is God's will or that His will always takes place. But that is not the case. According to Andrew Murray, God wills many blessings to His people which never come to them. The problem is that although He wills it most earnestly, they don't will it. Therefore, God has made much of the execution of His will dependent on the will or choice(s) of man.

Whether He miraculously intervenes in our life circumstances or not, God loves us. Our faith should never be conditional on how we think or hope God should act. And, yes, this is unreasonable as we know it. We certainly do not choose to be involved in tragedies, but we are still indirectly feeling the fallout of Adam and Eve's choices. Because God gives us the ability to choose, we are often at risk of feeling the consequences of others' painful, and at times, poor and unfair choices. If someone ever asks the "why" question, our most spiritual response could be "I do not know, but I do know He loves you in spite of what has happened."

It's best to move away from the unanswered "Whys" because they lose their relevancy. Unanswered whys, one of the biggest disputes between God and humanity, haunt too many people and hinder them from having a meaningful relationship with Him. Answers have a tendency to make us feel safe, and it is OK to ask why. Realize you may not get a satisfactory answer, however. Our faith becomes more poignant because we don't have the answers. To ask why is not a character or spiritual flaw; it merely reveals our humanness. This is best illustrated by Jesus' question while upon the Cross, "My God, my God, why have you forsaken me" (Matthew 27:46)?

Answers don't change what has occurred, and using human reason, even with an answer, we may still not agree or understand. If God wanted us to understand or know everything, He would have given us that ability. This is the essence of trust. Relentless trust in Him will slowly overcome His mystery and any injustice of human suffering.

In addition, answers may not necessarily bring any significant comfort because we need a Presence and the act(s) of healing more than we need a formal explanation. Taken in the appropriate context and timeline, emotional turmoil can be an opportunity for us to come closer to Him. In His time, our deepest scars can become our greatest gifts. Genesis 50:20 states, "You intended to harm me, but God intended it for good to accomplish what is now being done, the saving of many lives."

Endurance

"Consider it pure joy, my brothers, whenever you face trials of many kinds, because you know that the testing of your faith develops perseverance. Perseverance must finish its work so that you may be mature and complete, not lacking anything."

James 1:2-4

Endurance is a form of mental agility and offers a sense of permanence, firmness, or steadiness. Endurance implies "over a length of time." It is the ability to withstand hardship with composure. The Greek translation of perseverance is the quality which does not easily surrender to suffering circumstances, and is opposed to cowardice or prolonged despondency. When we endure, we reflect God's image. C. S. Lewis states, "If we have the will to walk, then God is pleased with our stumbles." Adversity would eventually give me the fuel to endure by allowing God to not only transform me but also my current circumstances.

Adversity forces us to dig deep and discover whether we are building, discovering, or losing our backbone. It can help move us out of our obstinacy and indifference. It takes endurance for us to bear the "thorns" in our lives. Instead of solely focusing on having them removed, we may need to be content to pray for the strength and wisdom to continue to bear them. The fact that Paul's thorn has never been identified is actually a blessing for us. All persons have a thorn if they are fortunate enough to find it. My once painful memories are now viewed from the perspective of a "welcomed" thorn because they help maintain my vigilance upon Him. There is no haunting to the memories, for they have been stripped of their negative, compulsive power.

I now try to use the memories in a different way to view them from a different perspective. Sometimes I do well. Sometimes I don't. I'm learning to be more patient and more willing to learn from my thorn's pain. Before, my natural tendency was to hastily remove it without regard to what I may have learned from it. Yet then, and now, I'm not overly thrilled at the prospect of being a student in the classroom of emotional pain. This remains a growing edge for me. We often do not exercise the patience or willingness to learn from or endure the thorn's pain. Our natural tendency is to hastily remove it.

In life, we are running a marathon, not a wind sprint. We need a sense of pace. Because of my present day profession as a mental health counselor combined with my past experiences, I am very aware that I am prone and/or at high risk for burnout and depression. I am very conscious of my personal boundaries, sometimes to a fault. We are to run with endurance by setting specific goals and envisioning our prize at the finish line as we experience the supernatural grace of God. Goals encourage us to carry on. Someone once said, "If you aim at nothing, you will hit it every single time." We increase our endurance by various forms of exercise. Trials, hopes, joys, and encouragement are what exercise our endurance the most. Spiritual transformation requires endurance. Revelation 3:10 promises, "Since you have kept my command to endure patiently, I will also keep you..."

Furthermore, we are to seek and teach endurance (I Timothy 6:11, Titus 2:2). Teaching others is a way to foster obedience. One of the best means to nurture our relationship with Christ is through rigorous and disciplined study of the Bible. One finds a disciple in discipline. All formal discipleship requires is an open Bible and heart. Brennan Manning states, "child-like surrender in trust is the defining spirit of authentic discipleship." The greatest attribute to teach a person or ourselves is to develop the presence of mind to look to God in all things. Nothing disciplines us more than service to our fellow man. We are called to servanthood not only to help others, but also because of what it does to us spiritually.

One of the greatest human examples of endurance is Abraham Lincoln. His life story is an amazing example of how grace can fuel our motivation to endure. Born into poverty in 1809, Lincoln faced numerous trials throughout his life. He could have quit many times, but because he didn't, he became one of the greatest Presidents of our country.

Consider:

1816: His family was forced out of their home. He had to work to support them.

1818: His mother died.

1831: He failed in business.

1832: He ran for the state legislature. He LOST.

1832: He also lost his job. He wanted to go to law school but couldn't get in.

1833: He borrowed some money from a friend to begin a business and by the end of the year, he was bankrupt. He spent 17 years of his life paying off his debt.

1834: He ran for state legislature again. He WON.

1835: He was engaged to be married. His fiancé died and his heart was broken.

1836: He had a total nervous breakdown and was in bed

for six months.

1838: He sought to become speaker of the state legislature. He LOST.

1840: He sought to become elector. He LOST.

1843: He ran for Congress. He LOST.

1846: He ran for Congress again. He WON and went to Washington.

1848: He ran for re-election to Congress. He LOST.

1849: He sought the job of land officer in his home state. He LOST.

1850: His three year old son, Eddie, died of tuberculosis.

1854: He ran for Senate of the United States. He LOST.

1856: He sought the Vice-Presidential nomination at his party's convention. He LOST. (He received less than a hundred votes.)

1858: He ran for U. S. Senate again. Again he LOST.

1860: He was ELECTED PRESIDENT OF THE UNITED STATES.

1862: His 11-year-old son, Willie, died of typhoid fever.

1865: At the age of 56, he was assassinated.

> "For though a righteous man falls seven times, he rises again..."
>
> Proverbs 24:16

Spiritual endurance gives a person the wherewithal to know when he needs a gentle touch and at other times a swift-kick. As unbearable as it can feel, we need to see through the adversity. Remember the hospitalized man in the movie, *Patch Adams*? He would hold up four fingers on one hand and ask how many fingers you could see. If you only saw four, the problem was that you were strictly focused on the problem (fingers). But if you looked and focused beyond the problem (past and through the fingers and across the room), you could see the number of fingers had doubled to eight. The increased number of fingers can represent our increased blessings with Christ when we choose to endure. A good rule of thumb is no matter how agonizing our circumstance(s) are or can be, it is always too early to quit, yet it is never too late to begin. Even though we can't go back to make a fresh start, we can always make a brand new ending. In the words of Winston Churchill, "If you're going through hell, keep going."

Enduring is much more than merely existing. To only exist is to live at an inferior level. The abundant life and joy are found through change. While patience generally refers to our response to people, endurance refers to our response to tough circumstances. God patiently endures our behavior; He has virtually no limits on His grace and patience. The cock crowed three times for Peter, and this was the turning point in his life. Previously, Peter had not been brought to the end of himself. Only after he became broken and wept, did his great transformation come (Luke 22:54-62).

Contentment

"I have learned to be content whatever the circumstances. I know what it is to be in need, and I know what it is to have plenty. I have learned the secret of being content in any and every situation, whether well fed or hungry, whether living in plenty or in want. I can do everything through him who gives me strength."

Philippians 4:11-13

Peace finds contentment in all circumstances; contentment not for the circumstances, but in them, or in spite of them. Peace is our poise and demeanor during times of crisis and stress. It gives us the needed calm throughout the tough times. 1 Thessalonians 5:18 tells us to, "Give thanks in all circumstances, for this is God's will for you in Christ Jesus."

"Giving thanks" is God's will, but not necessarily for the circumstance in which we may currently find ourselves. This was exemplified by the peace Paul felt and experienced from within his prison cell. The cell itself and his impending death had become insignificant. God is glorified in our gratitude, even in the most trying of times. He is there when His children face life's darkest valleys. C.S. Lewis tells us, "God whispers to us in our pleasure, speaks in our conscience, but shouts in our pain." It is a formidable task to be content because there is nothing in this world which will satisfy what we yearn for the most: unconditional love, purpose and meaning. Our personal relationship with God is the only cause of our contentment. Lewis goes on to say, "the very nature of joy makes nonsense of our common distinction between having and wanting."

Discontentment is defined by many as: what we do for God is too much and what He does for us is too little. For the longest time, I had firmly settled on the latter. But even dissatisfaction can be a form of God's grace, because it tells us there is something more. Hopefully it creates a new thirst for His Spirit.

On the other hand, contentment is a quality of life not found in great wealth but in having few wants. Contentment is properly valuing what we have, more than defining ourselves by what we lack. It is a form of self-discipline which limits our requirements, desires, or actions. People with vast material wealth are often the most miserable. Rockefeller once said the poorest people he ever saw were the ones who had nothing but money. Carnegie also stated that he seldom saw a rich man smile. Being able and willing to do without is real power.

Acceptance, forgiveness, and peace are discovered only within an eternal perspective. Although the past can't be changed, our perspective can. Indeed, it is harder to let go of the past when nothing has been learned from it. Hanging on to the past prevents us from envisioning an expanding range of possibilities far beyond the perceptions we have created from our prior experiences. Faith isn't about what we have done, but it is what we believe now. The eventual consequence of our faith is peace. John 14:27 reminds us, "Peace I leave with you; my peace I give you. I do not give to you as the world gives."

- 15 -

GIVING MEANING TO OUR SUFFERING

"In bringing many sons to glory, it was fitting that God, for whom and through whom everything exists, should make the author of their salvation perfect through suffering."

Hebrews 2:10

According to Viktor Frankl in his classic, *Man's Search for Meaning*, "The problem is that people have enough to live by but nothing to live for, they have the means but no meaning."[1] Rather than focusing on what is missing in our lives, which is how many people define themselves, we need to focus on what is left...God's love for us. The greatest disease known to man is not heart disease or cancer; it is the disease of feeling unloved. Make no mistake: Christ has an intense and ongoing affection for you.

Our future is far more important than the past. Frankl lost all of his immediate family members (the odds of surviving were one in twenty-eight) in the concentration camps, but he discovered the Nazis couldn't take away his attitude and hope. This realization kept him alive and sane through the survival of four camps. Frankl's experiences tell us that our attitude and hope are the only things we can freely choose to give away.

Our main concerns should not be limited to gaining pleasure or strictly in avoiding pain, but rather in finding meaning. Frankl makes clear that in no way is suffering necessary to find meaning. "Meaning is possible in spite of suffering. Human life, under any circumstances, never ceases to have meaning. This infinite meaning of life includes suffering, privation, and death."[2]

A Dutch Jew named Etty Hillesum, who died in a camp, saw the same thing. In her work entitled, *An Interrupted Life: The Diaries,* she writes: "There is a limit to suffering, perhaps no human being is given more than he can shoulder—beyond a certain point we just die. People are dying here even now of a broken spirit, because they can no longer find any meaning in life, young people. The old ones are rooted in firmer soil and accept their fate with dignity and calm. You see many different sets of people here and so many attitudes to the hardest ultimate questions."[3]

Compassionate Closure

Closure is described as a state of confinement or conclusion. In dealing with adversity, closure is a very important aspect in being able to move on with life. Is real closure possible? The concept has some symbolic value in regard to integrating and managing past issues, and the setting of appropriate emotional boundaries. Although closure has its place in certain dynamics, we should not want or need complete closure. Remember the thorn. With a sense of closure, we may lose its full impact. We should never forget the despair of being lost. This memory is not to honor or worship our despair, but a way to always be aware of it in order to help us remain grounded. Our poor memory can create a sense of smugness.

Maybe, like healing and sanctification, closure is best described as a lifelong process. Both good and bad memories can be of relative worth. In my understanding of closure, I am in the process of closing certain chapters of my life, but the book is far from complete. Memories give me the ability to reference previous chapters if and when the need arises. A more viable goal for me, rather than closure from a past experience, may be how close I can draw toward Christ.

Adversity is always an affirming tool when entrusted to Christ. Our response to adversity is what makes suffering valuable. Some people pull themselves back together (being broken to become whole) and go on to learn whatever God wants to teach them, in spite of the adversity not originally being His will. Unfortunately, others never recuperate, and they slowly disintegrate into ashes of hurt.

Through all his trials, Joseph learned to trust, "Not that God would prevent hardship, but that He would redeem even the hardship," Phillip Yancey suggests.[4] Daniel was allowed into the lion's den and then made able to leave through his deep faith. Wisdom may often need to be experienced in order to be learned. The ultimate goal of God in adversity is to increase our depth of trust in Him by keeping focused on His ability. God purifies our trust through trials. Often, trust begins to form on the far, dark, lonely side of tragedy. In the words of Walter Burghardt, "Only trust makes evil endurable." Trust and patience were no longer my opponents. They were now welcomed team mates that enriched my team's chemistry.

The fact that more joy and adversity is ahead can help keep us dependent on the sufficiency of Christ. We need to focus on His ability rather than on our adversity. Joy and suffering guide us on our journey to wholeness, and we need to accept both as inevitable companions. Although God never wastes pain, we do. Christ wants to walk with us through the recovery from life's hurts to experience new joys. Nothing could be worse than a scar-filled life with virtually nothing to show for it.

The Thirst for Time

Time can be a misguided excuse to avoid the strenuous work of grief and recovery. Time per se does not heal a thing. It is the quality of what we do in the interval which matters. Although it does take time to heal, the phrase, "Time heals all wounds" is a fallacy. Just ask any bitter person you know. "In God's time" is when the adversity has served its divine purpose. Similarly, Frankl makes clear, "Suffering ceases to be suffering at the moment it finds meaning."[5] Although God doesn't necessarily create or cause adversity, He will always reveal His eternal and redemptive purpose within it. Even though healing is a lifelong process, there is a point where we become stronger, yet are still healing. This is similar to when we break a bone. After healing, the point of the break is actually stronger than the original bone.

Service and Ministry

"Each one should use whatever gift he has received to serve others, faithfully administering God's grace in its various forms."

I Peter 4:10

We need to follow God along the entire path. Just being OK or merely getting back to where we were before the adversity is far too limiting for God and ourselves. God doesn't want us to settle with just breaking even. What would be the value of the adversity? The gist is we didn't come through adversity not to use it for the sake of others. I would need to live my wounds. Through all my joys and trials, God cultivated me for His ministry. He has called all of us to be a ministers in some capacity, regardless of our vocations. There are certain tasks that only you can do. We are not only ministers, but we can also be witnesses who are more than willing to testify concerning God's goodness.

Personal Application

I was discharged from the state hospital on Father's Day weekend. It was a most fitting timeline. Most of my formal treatment while at the state hospital emphasized time. Other than counseling and trying new or different medications, time and process was a premium for me. I needed time to reflect, think, pray, ponder, and determine what I was going to do for the rest of my life.

Looking back, if His Spirit hadn't led me to the chapel, I'm afraid I may still be hospitalized. Indifference is what I saw in many patients and staff members. I felt many people had accepted their fate and had not challenged themselves to the degree they could have.

My experience there would later remind me of Clifford Beers' book, *A Mind That Found Itself.* The book gives a classic account of the author's mental illness and how he gradually lost touch with reality. Although he was brutalized by his treatment, he would still claim eventual recovery. His story was one of triumph of the human spirit. My experience pales in comparison to Beers', and I was certainly not mistreated by anyone, but I would like to think my recovery was more of the

Holy Spirit's triumph over my own circumstances and humanness. Once Beers recovered from his illness, he began a lifelong mission to overhaul the care and treatment of the mentally ill. Once I recovered from my woes, I, too, would want to help people in the midst of their suffering.

That fall, I returned to college and finally graduated the following May. Several churches throughout the area to ask me to share my experience. I was being led to enter the ministry in some capacity, yet I rationalized, denied, and ran from His call. How vain it was to think I could outrun God; I wonder if I was ever winning or if God was ever running.

During a period of just over seven years, an inner tension kept pulling me away from the corporate world of being a Wal-mart store manager and into God's ministry. The talents and skills God had given me through the scars were not being fully utilized. Part of the desire to be successful in the business world was to prove to others and myself that I was now all right. But a lifestyle of trying to prove anything is not a Godly lifestyle. For our family, a total surrender and dependence on God included my vocation. There were no audible voices or commands, but an inner, unshakeable discernment and confidence.

Ironically, my formal calling may have started when I was told of Tina's death. There was definitely a message in "Christmas Day." Having been raised in an alcoholic atmosphere was an ingredient, too. Through several negative key aspects of life, God enabled me to see the positive alternatives in trying to cope, in order one day to help bring comfort to others. Gracious people allowed me to be a part of their journey, and now I was led to do the same. God wanted to give His purpose to my suffering, for there was a divine reason for me to have lived through the accident. According to Marcel Proust,

"We are healed of suffering only by experiencing it to the fullest."

For many courageous people, pastoral counseling can be a way to bring further wholeness into their lives. In order for someone to genuinely comfort, he must have been himself comforted by the Holy Comforter. Accordingly, we cannot be messengers of divine grace to a person without having benefited from it ourselves. The task of helping restore dignity to a broken heart is the truest meaning of the counseling process. Healing begins the moment we take the first step. With each successive step we are assured that, "He will wipe every tear from their eyes. There will be no more death or mourning or crying or pain, for the old order of things has passed away" (Revelation 21:4).

Final Reflections

Because of Tina's death on Christmas Day, Jesus' birth has even more meaning. Christmas is hope in the midst of tragedy. Jesus' birth, assures us that life is stronger than death, and that good overcomes evil. Love never fails and tragedy will never have the last word. The miracle of Christmas wasn't only that a child had been born to us, but that God's Son would survive all the various forms of hell we could possibly give him in order to live as our example. Christmas is a season to spread the joy that has overcome heartache and tragedy. His birth marks the beginning of His holy and whole message. For me, His very manger repaired what guilt and shame had broken. Christmas tells us that we will never be without hope or purpose again. Hope eventually comes to terms with tragedy. For our family, an example of finding new meaning in the midst of tragedy, was the baptism of our infant daughter, Sarah, on Christmas Day, 1994.

Jesus' suffering and death were also integral parts of His earthly life. All three occasions (His birth, His suffering and death, and His Resurrection) are of equal importance and are connected or His message is lost. The message is whole, although it isn't always pretty. It includes the dark and gruesome side of suffering. Similarly, we need to accept all the various components in our lives, including the most ugly and unpleasant one(s), as well as His love, grace, and forgiveness. In essence, our journey can actually parallel His.

The detours of adversity are occasions to get out of our driver's seat, and are opportunities to go new places with God, once we surrender to Him. A detour signals a needed change in our present course. For me, it was the ultimate challenge to yield, give up my driver's seat, and then give God the right-of-way.

Today, I often reflect on the plight of Tina's family. It's always there. When visiting my parents' graves, it's impossible not to think of them. Tina, her father, and her sister are all buried about thirty yards from my parents in a nearby national military cemetery. The twists and turns in life have definitely evolved into a full circle experience.

I've been a pastoral counselor for over thirteen years now, and this time has been the best of my life, although I continue to have the ups and downs and struggles of life that we all have. God has blessed me with a great family and a most meaningful vocation. As Henri Nouwen states, "Ministry can indeed be a witness to the living truth that the wound, which causes us to suffer now, will be revealed to us later as the place where God intimated His new creation."[6] Joan Borysenko says we can have hope when we have reached the darkest point of our spiritual pilgrimage because we know from the stories of people who have walked before us that dawn is at hand. And although we may feel that we are following a narrow and perilous path alone, it has been walked numerous times before. We have never been, nor will we ever be, alone.

Invite or challenge yourself and others; find one person who has genuinely sought God's grace and forgiveness and didn't receive it. Under God's will, discover your destiny as you continue to be the person you are becoming. God is not through with you yet. Expect to be changed and embrace the relationship you were created for. Between guilt and grace, God chose grace. What will be your choice?

Be free my friend.

"First keep peace within yourself, then you can also bring peace to others."

Thomas A. Kempis

The Serenity Prayer

God, grant me the SERENITY to accept the things that I cannot change....COURAGE to change the things that I can....and the WISDOM to know the difference. Living one day at a time, enjoying one moment at a time, ACCEPTING hardship as the pathway to PEACE. Taking, as Jesus did, this sinful world as it is, not as I would have it. TRUSTING that He will make all things right if I surrender to His will. That I may be reasonably happy in this life, and supremely happy with Him forever in the next.

Amen

Slow Me Down, Lord Jesus

Slow me down Lord.
Ease the pounding of my heart by the quieting of my mind.
Steady my hurried pace with a vision of your eternal glory.
Give me, amid the confusion of the day, the calmness of your presence.
Break the tensions of my nerves and muscles with the soothing experiences of your presence.

Help me to know the magical, restoring power of sleep.
Teach me the art of taking minute vacations—of slowing down to look at a flower;
To chat with a friend;
To pat a dog;
To read the Bible;
To pray to you.

Slow me down, Lord, and inspire me to send my roots deep into the soil of life's enduring values that I may grow in Your grace.
Thank you Lord, Jesus.

Author Unknown

NOTES

Chapter 1:
1. Tournier, Paul, *Guilt and Grace,* Harper Row Publishers, 1962. p.139.

Chapter 2:
1. Spurgeon, Charles, *Grace Abounding in a Believer's Life,* Emerald Books, Lynnwood, WA. 1994. p.131.
2. Beker, F. Christian, *Suffering and Hope,* Eerdman's Publishing Company, 1987. p.94.

Chapter 3:
1. Henslin, Earl R., *Forgiven and Free,* Thomas Nelson, Nashville, 1991. p.139.
2. Roberts, Ted, *Pure Desire,* Ventura, CA: Regal, 1999. p.128.

Chapter 6:
1. Dobson, James, *Emotions, Can You Trust Them?* Ventura, CA: Regal Books, 1980, p.17.
2. Nesbitt, Maurice, *Where No Fear Was,* New York: Seaberg Press, 1981. pp. 35, 49.
3. Tournier, Paul, p. 81.
4. Madden, Myron, *The Power to Bless,* Insight Press, New Orleans, LA. 1999.
5. Tournier, Paul, p. 67.
6. Madden, Myron, *The Power to Bless,* Insight Press, New Orleans, LA. 1999. p. 70.

Chapter 7:
1. Kushner, Harold, *How Good Do We Have To Be?,* Back Bay Books, 1996. p.53.
2. Witkin, Georgia, *Passions: How to Manage Despair, Fear, Rage and Guilt and Heighten Your Capacity for Joy, Love, Hope and Awe,* New York: Villard/Random House, 1992. p.96.
3. Narramore, Bruce and Counts, Bill, *Freedom from Guilt,* Harvest House Publishers, Eugene, OR. 1974. p.113.

4. Smedes, Lewis, *Shame and Grace*, Harper San Francisco, New York, NY. Reprint Edition, 1993. p.80.

Chapter 8:
1. Bonhoeffer, Dietrich, *Life Together*, San Francisco: Harper Row, 1954. p.113.
2. Foster, Richard, *Celebration of Discipline*, Harper & Row Publishers, New York, NY. 1988. p. 80.
3. Manning, Brennan, *Ruthless Trust*, Harper San Francisco, 2000. p.120.
4. Mason, Mike, *The Mystery of Marriage*, Portland: Multnomah Press, 1985. p.41.

Chapter 9:
1. Madden, Myron, p.13.
2. Lake, Frank, *Clinical Theology*, London: Darton, Longman & Todd, 1966, pp. 1114-15.
3. Author Unknown.

Chapter 10:
1. Barnhouse, Donald Grey, *Romans, Man's Ruin*, Vol. 1, Grand Rapids, Wm. B. Eerdman's Publishing Company, 1952. p.72.
2. Augsburger, David, *Helping People Forgive*, Westminster John Knox Press, Louisville, KY. 1996. p.120.
3. Alcorn, Randy, *The Grace and Truth Paradox*, Multnomah Publishers, 2003. p.29.
4. Sproul, R. C., *Suffering and Merit? Table Talk Magazine*, Orlando, FL: Ligonier Ministries, Vol.13, No. 1, 1989. p.5.
5. Calvin, John, *Calvin's New Testament Commentaries*, Vol. 10. The Second Epistle of Paul the Apostle to the Corinthians and the Epistles to Timothy, Titus, and Philemon. pp.32-33.
6. Bridges, Jerry, *Transforming Grace*, Navpress, Colorado Springs, CO., 1991. p.157.
7. Tozer, A.W., *The Pursuit of God*, Christians Publications, Inc. Camp Hill, PA., 1982. p.113.

8. Viorst, Judith, *Necessary Losses,* Fawcett Gold Medal, New York, 1986. p.138.

Chapter 11:
1. Author Unknown
2. Mayfield, James, *Discovering Grace in Grief,* Upper Room Books, 1994, p.74.
3. Seamands, David, *The Healing of Damaged Emotions,* Victor Books, Wheaton, IL, 1989. p.109.
4. Kalas, Ellsworth, *Parables From the Backside,* Abingdon Press, Nashville, TN, 1992. p.66.

Chapter 12:
1. Augsburger, David, *The Freedom of Forgiveness,* Moody Press, Chicago, IL. 1970. p.46.
2. Neill, Stephen, *A Genuinely Human Existence,* Doubleday & Co./Constable, Garden City, N.Y., and London, 1959. pp. 210-11.
3. Henslin, Earl R., p.153.
4. Augsburger, David, *Helping People Forgive,* Westminster John Knox Press, Louisville, KY. p. 28.
5. Seamands, Steve, *Wounds that Heal,* Intervarsity Press, Downers Grove, IL, 2003, p.141.
6. Lewis, C.S., *The Weight of Glory,* Macmillan Company, New York, NY, 1949. p.1-2.
7. Schreiter, Robert J., *Reconciliation,* Maryknoll, N.Y., Orbis Books. 1992. p.43.
8. Elizondo, Virgil, *I Forgive But I Do Not Forget,* Edinburgh: T. & T. Clark. 1986. p. 70.
9. Author Unknown.
10. Author Unknown.
11. Nouwen, Henri, *The Way of the Heart,* Ballatine Books, New York, 1981. p.18.

Chapter 13:
1. Seamands, Steve, pp.11-12.
2. Lake, Frank, *Clinical Theology,* London: Darton, Longman & Todd, 1996 pp. xxx, xxii.

3. Seamands, David, *The Healing of Damaged Emotions,* Victor Books, Wheaton, IL 1989. p.22.
4. Irving, Washington, American writer (1783-1859).
5. Tozer, A.W., *Total Commitment,* Decision, August 1963, p. 4.
6. Bonhoeffer, Dietrich, *Life Together,* San Francisco: Harper Row, 1954. p.118-119.

Chapter 14:
1. Seamands, David, *The Healing of Damaged Emotions,* p.98.
2. Craigie, P.C., *The New International Commentary on the Old Testament,* Wm.B. Eerdman's Publishing Company, 1976. p.146.

Chapter 15:
1. Frankl, Viktor, *Man's Search for Meaning,* Simon and Schuster, Inc., 1984. p.142.
2. Frankl, Viktor, p.117.
3. Hillesum, Etty, *An Interrupted Life: The Diaries,* 1941-1943. Owl Books, New York, NY. 1996. p.247.
4. Yancey, Phillip, *Disappointment with God,* Zondervan, 1988. p.67.
5. Frankl, Viktor, p. 117.
6. Nouwen, Henri, *The Wounded Healer,* Image Books, Garden City, N.Y., 1979. p.9.

BIBLIOGRAPHY

Albers, Robert, *Shame*, Haworth Pastoral Press, 1995.

Alcorn, Randy, *The Grace and Truth Paradox*, Multnomah Publishers, 2003.

Augsburger, David, *Helping People Forgive*, Westminster John Knox Press, 1996.

Augsburger, David, *The Freedom of Forgiveness*, Moody Press, 1970.

Barnhouse, Donald Grey, *Romans, Man's Ruin*, Wm. B. Eerdman's Publishing, 1952.

Beker, F. Christian, *Suffering and Hope*, Wm. B. Eerdman's Publishing Company, 1987.

Berke, Joseph H., *Shame and Envy*, Guilford Press, 1987.

Blamires, Harry, *Recovering the Christian Mind*, Intervarsity Press, 1988.

Bonhoeffer, Dietrich, *Life Together*, Harper Row, 1954.

Bonhoeffer, Dietrich, *The Cost of Discipleship*, Macmillan, 1959.

Borysenko, Joan, *Guilt is the Teacher, Love is the Lesson*, Warner Books, 1991.

Bridges, Jerry, *Transforming Grace: Living Confidently in God's Unfailing Love*, Navpress, 1993.

Calvin, John, *Calvin's New Testament Commentaries*, Vol. 10.

Clapp, Rodney, "Shame Crucified," *Christianity Today*, March 11, 1991.

Cooke, Joseph R., *Free for the Taking*, Fleming Revell, 1975.

Craigie, P.C., *The New International Commentary on the Old Testament*, Wm. B. Eerdman's Publishing Company, 1976.

Danieli, Yael, *Psychoanalytic Psychology*, 1, 1984.

Dobson, James, *Emotions, Can You Trust Them?*, Regal Books, 1980.

Elizondo, Virgil, *I Forgive But I Do Not Forget*, T. & T. Clark, 1986.

Fossum, M., and Mason, M., *Facing Shame*, Norton, 1986.

Foster, Richard, *Celebration of Discipline*, Harper and Row, 1978.

Frankl, Viktor, *Man's Search for Meaning*, Simon and Schuster, Inc., 1984.

Henslin, Earl, R., *Forgiven and Free*, Thomas Nelson, 1991.

Hillesum, Etty, *An Interrupted Life: The Diaries*, 1941-1943.

Kaufman, Gershen, *Shame: The Power of Caring*, Schenkman Publishing, 1980.

Kushner, Harold, *How Good Do We Have to Be?*, Back Bay Books, 1996.

Lake, Frank, *Clinical Theology*, Darton, Longman & Todd, 1966.

Lewis, C.S., *Mere Christianity*, Macmillan Publishing Company, 1964.

Lewis, C.S., *The Weight of Glory*, Macmillan Company, 1949.

Madden, Myron, *The Power to Bless*, Insight Press, 1999.

Mason, Mike, *The Mystery of Marriage*, Multnomah Press, 1985.

Manning, Brennan, *Ruthless Trust*, Harper San Francisco, 2000.

Mayfield, James, *Discovering Grace in Grief*, Upper Room Books, 1994.

Narramore, Bruce, and Counts, Bill, *Freedom From Guilt*, House Publishers, 1974.

Neill, Stephen, *A Genuinely Human Existence*, Doubleday & Company, 1959.

Nesbitt, Maurice, *Where No Fear Was*, Seaberg Press, 1981.

Nouwen, Henri, *The Wounded Healer*, Doubleday Image Book, 1979.

Nouwen, Henri, *The Way of the Heart*, Ballantine Books, 1981.

Patton, John, *Is Human Forgiveness Possible?*, Abingdon Press, 1985.

Roberts, Ted, *Pure Desire*, Regal, 1999.

Schneider, Carl D., *Shame, Exposure, and Privacy*, Beacon Press, 1977.

Schreiter, Robert J., *Reconciliation*, Orbis Books, 1992.

Seamands, David, *The Healing of Damaged Emotions*, Victor Books, 1989.

Seamands, David, *If Only*, Victor Books, 1995.

Seamands, Stephen, *Wounds that Heal*, Intervarsity Press, 2003.

Smedes, Lewis, *Shame and Grace*, Harper San Francisco, 1993.

Sproul, R. C., *Suffering and Merit?*, Ligonier Ministries, 1989.

Spurgeon, Charles, *Grace Abounding in a Believer's Life*, Emerald Books, 1994.

Tournier, Paul, *Guilt and Grace*, Harper Row Publishers, 1962.

Tozer, A. W., *Total Commitment*, Decision, 1963.

Tozer, A. W., *The Pursuit of God*, Christian Publications, 1982.

Viorst, Judith, *Necessary Losses*, Fawcett Gold Medal, 1986.

Witkin, Georgia, *Passions: How to Manage Despair, Fear, Rage and Guilt and Heighten Your Capacity for Joy, Love, Hope and Awe*, Villard/Random House, 1992.

Yancey, Phillip, *Disappointment with God*, Zondervan, 1988.

ABOUT THE AUTHOR

Rev. Hiram Johnson, LCSW, BCD, graduated from Asbury Theological Seminary with the MA degree in parish counseling, the University of Kentucky with the MSW degree (master's, social work), and Florida State University with the B.S. degree in management. He is an ordained Deacon in the United Methodist Church for the Alabama-West Florida Conference and is currently appointed beyond the local church to Crossway Counseling Center, a private practice setting in Daphne, Alabama.

Hiram is also a Board Certified Diplomate in his discipline of clinical social work and is licensed in both Alabama and Florida. He and his wife, Jill, and two daughters, Hannah and Sarah, currently reside in Fairhope, Alabama.

To contact Hiram Johnson
regarding speaking engagements,
email him at
JJFSUFAN@aol.com

— To Order —

Tragic Redemption: Healing the Guilt and Shame

by Hiram Johnson

If unavailable at your favorite bookstore,
Langmarc Publishing will fill
your order within 24 hours.

— Postal Orders —
LangMarc Publishing
P.O. Box 90488
Austin, Texas 78709-0488

or call 1-800-864-1648
or online www.langmarc.com

Tragic Redemption
USA: $14.95 + $3 postage
Canada: $18.95 + $5 postage

Send _____ copies of *Tragic Redemption* $14.95

Shipping   3.00

TX res. 8.25%_____

Amount of Sale _____

Send to: _____

_____

_____

Phone: _____

Check enclosed: _____

Credit Card # _____

Expiration: _____ Code: _____

Printed in the United States
219091BV00001B/1/P